Sum Fun
Maths Assessment

Years 1–2
Maths Assessment Puzzles
for the
2014 Curriculum

Katherine Bennett

Brilliant
PUBLICATIONS

We hope you and your pupils enjoy solving the maths puzzles in this book. Brilliant Publications publishes other books for maths and maths problems. To find out more details on any of the titles listed below, please log onto our website: www.brilliantpublications.co.uk.

Maths Problem Solving Year 1   978-1-903853-74-0
Maths Problem Solving Year 2   978-1-903853-75-7
Maths Problem Solving Year 3   978-1-903853-76-4
Maths Problem Solving Year 4   978-1-903853-77-1
Maths Problem Solving Year 5   978-1-903853-78-8
Maths Problem Solving Year 6   978-1-903853-79-5

Maths Problems and Investigations 5–7 year olds   978-0-85747-626-5
Maths Problems and Investigations 7–9 year olds   978-0-85747-627-2
Maths Problems and Investigations 9–11 year olds   978-0-85747-628-9

The Mighty Multiples Times Table Challenge   978-0-85747-629-6

Published by Brilliant Publications
Unit 10
Sparrow Hall Farm
Edlesborough
Dunstable
Bedfordshire
LU6 2ES, UK

E-mail:
  info@brilliantpublications.co.uk
Website:
  www.brilliantpublications.co.uk
Tel: 01525 222292

The name Brilliant Publications and the logo are registered trademarks.

Written by Katherine Bennett
Illustrated by Cathy Hughes
Front cover illustration by Cathy Hughes

© Text Katherine Bennett 2014
© Design Brilliant Publications 2014

Printed ISBN 978-1-78317-083-8
e-book ISBN 978-1-78317-088-3

First printed and published in the UK in 2014

Contents

Introduction

The aim of the 'Sum Fun' series is to enable teachers to gather evidence and assess children's learning in maths.

Linked to year group objectives from the new September 2014 curriculum, each fun activity sheet requires pupils to use their mathematical skills to solve a series of questions. They must then use the answers to 'crack the code' and find the solutions to silly jokes, puns and riddles. The activities use Assessment for Learning techniques, such as child friendly 'I can ...' statements at the top of each sheet, so that pupils can be clear about the learning objective; they also encourage self-assessment because if a solution doesn't make sense, pupils will need to spot and correct their mistakes. Quick reference answer pages are provided for the teacher at the back of the book, or to enable pupils to self-mark. There are several sheets per objective so that each one can be tested at different points in the year if necessary, without repetition of the same questions and jokes. This could be at the end of a unit of work, or as a one-off assessment task. The assessment checklist on page 97 will help you to keep track of children's progress.

The activities are in a fun format that children soon become familiar with and look forward to solving, promoting high levels of pupil engagement. Children are motivated by the fun element of the jokes and will compete to be the first to get the answer!

As well as an assessment tool, the sheets can be used as independent tasks in everyday lessons. They are clearly linked to year group objectives from the new curriculum, providing an easy way of differentiating group or individual activities without any extra work for the class teacher! They make good whole class starter or plenary activities on an interactive whiteboard, or could just be used as fun 'time fillers'!

Counting forwards and backwards in ones (1)

Learning objectives
I can count forwards and backwards in ones.
I can count up to and across 100.

To solve the jokes, work out the number that comes next and write it in the circle. Then use the grid to find the letter that goes with each answer and write it on the line. The first one is done for you!

102	98	100	19	71	60	40	80	101	66	99	29
U	P	A	T	C	H	O	E	R	M	L	N

What did the dog wear to go cycling?

A / _ _ _ _ - _ _ _ _ !

97, 98, 99, (**100**)

63, 62, 61, ◯   77, 78, 79, ◯   102, 101, 100, ◯ –

63, 64, 65, ◯   99, 100, 101, ◯   22, 21, 20 ◯   16, 17, 18, ◯

What do dogs eat at the cinema?

_ _ _ _ - _ _ _ _ !

95, 96, 97, ◯   105, 104, 103, ◯   101, 100, 99, ◯ –

68, 69, 70, ◯   37, 38, 39, ◯   98, 99, 100, ◯   32, 31, 30, ◯

Year 1 – Number and place value
• *Count to and across 100, forwards and backwards, beginning with 0 or 1, or from any given number.*

Counting forwards and backwards in ones (2)

Learning objectives
I can count forwards and backwards in ones.
I can count up to and across 100.

To solve the jokes, work out the number that comes next and write it in the circle. Then use the grid to find the letter that goes with each answer and write it on the line. The first one is done for you!

70	80	39	100	99	29	59	19	50
T	A	S	D	E	Y	B	N	O

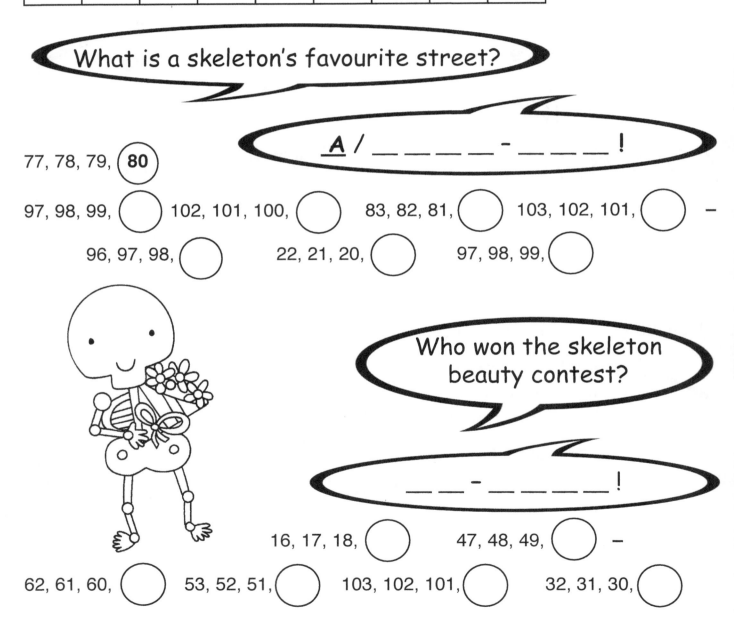

What is a skeleton's favourite street?

A / _ _ _ _ _ - _ _ _ _ !

77, 78, 79, (**80**)

97, 98, 99, ◯   102, 101, 100, ◯   83, 82, 81, ◯   103, 102, 101, ◯   –

96, 97, 98, ◯   22, 21, 20, ◯   97, 98, 99, ◯

Who won the skeleton beauty contest?

_ _ _ - _ _ _ _ !

16, 17, 18, ◯   47, 48, 49, ◯   –

62, 61, 60, ◯   53, 52, 51, ◯   103, 102, 101, ◯   32, 31, 30, ◯

Year 1 – Number and place value
• *Count to and across 100, forwards and backwards, beginning with 0 or 1, or from any given number.*

Counting forwards and backwards in ones (3)

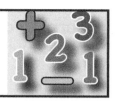

To solve the jokes, work out the number that comes next and write it in the circle. Then use the grid to find the letter that goes with each answer and write it on the line. The first one is done for you!

99	68	49	100	59	40	19	70	101	80
A	N	H	F	R	T	I	S	L	K

What did the fish use to blow up a building?

A / _ _ _ _ _ _ - _ _ _ _ _ _ !

96, 97, 98, (**99**)

97, 98, 99, ◯   16, 17, 18, ◯   67, 68, 69, ◯   52, 51, 50, ◯   –

37, 38, 39, ◯   102, 101, 100, ◯   71, 70, 69, ◯   83, 82, 81, ◯

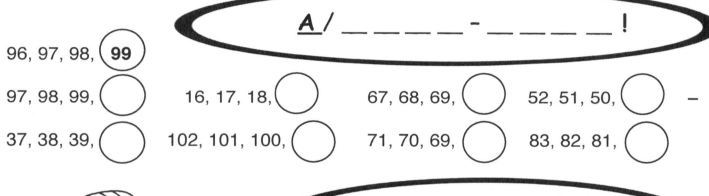

What do you get if you cross a haddock with a steamroller?

_ _ / _ _ _ _ _ / _ _ _ _ _ !

96, 97, 98, ◯

103, 102, 101, ◯   98, 99, 100, ◯   96, 97, 98, ◯   43, 42, 41, ◯

97, 98, 99, ◯   22, 21, 20, ◯   73, 72, 71, ◯   46, 47, 48, ◯

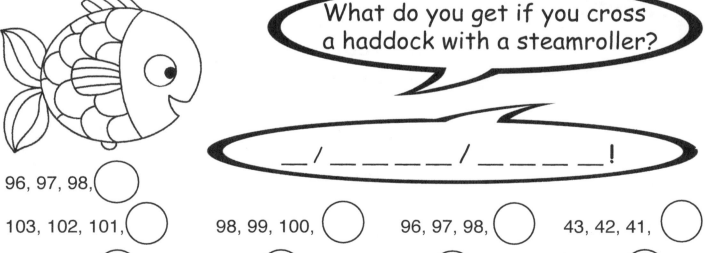

Year 1 – Number and place value
- *Count to and across 100, forwards and backwards, beginning with 0 or 1, or from any given number.*

Counting in multiples of 2, 5 and 10 (1)

Learning objectives
I can count forward in 2s, 5s and 10s.

To solve the jokes, work out the number that comes next and write it in the circle. Then use the grid to find the letter that goes with each answer and write it on the line. The first one is done for you!

12	60	70	58	40	50	16	30	90	20
C	Y	D	E	O	B	U	A	R	L

What's black when you buy it, red when you use it and grey when you throw it away?

<u>C</u> _ _ _ _ !

4, 8, 10, **(12)**   10, 20, 30, ◯   15, 20, 25, ◯   14, 16, 18, ◯

What has one head and four legs, but only one foot?

_ _ _ _ _ / _ _ _ _ !

30, 40, 50, ◯   25, 30, 35, ◯   10, 12, 14, ◯   60, 70, 80, ◯

35, 40, 45, ◯   52, 54, 56, ◯   40, 50, 60, ◯

Year 1 – Number and place value
· *Count, read and write numbers to 100 in numerals; count in multiples of twos, fives and tens.*

Counting in multiples of 2, 5 and 10 (2)

Learning objectives
I can count forward in 2s, 5s and 10s.

To solve the jokes, work out the number that comes next and write it in the circle. Then use the grid to find the letter that goes with each answer and write it on the line. The first one is done for you!

28	58	34	80	90	12	40	22	60	70
S	L	R	N	I	M	A	E	B	P

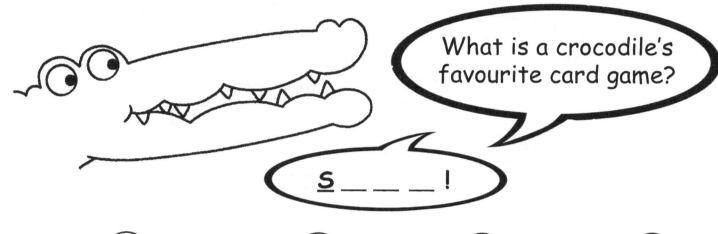

What is a crocodile's favourite card game?

S _ _ _ !

22, 24, 26, (28)   50, 60, 70, ◯   25, 30, 35, ◯   55, 60, 65, ◯

What do you call a sheep with fangs?

_ / _ _ _ _ - _ _ _ _ !

10, 20, 30, ◯

52, 54, 56, ◯   25, 30, 35, ◯   6, 8, 10, ◯   30, 40, 50, ◯

40, 50, 60, ◯   75, 80, 85, ◯   28, 30, 32, ◯   16, 18, 20, ◯

Year 1 – Number and place value
- Count, read and write numbers to 100 in numerals; count in multiples of twos, fives and tens.

Counting in multiples of 2, 5 and 10 (3)

Learning objectives
I can count forward in 2s, 5s and 10s.

To solve the jokes, work out the number that comes next and write it in the circle. Then use the grid to find the letter that goes with each answer and write it on the line. The first one is done for you!

40	30	50	45	90	80	35	60	70	100	23	22	44
P	Y	M	S	T	I	R	H	A	E	C	N	D

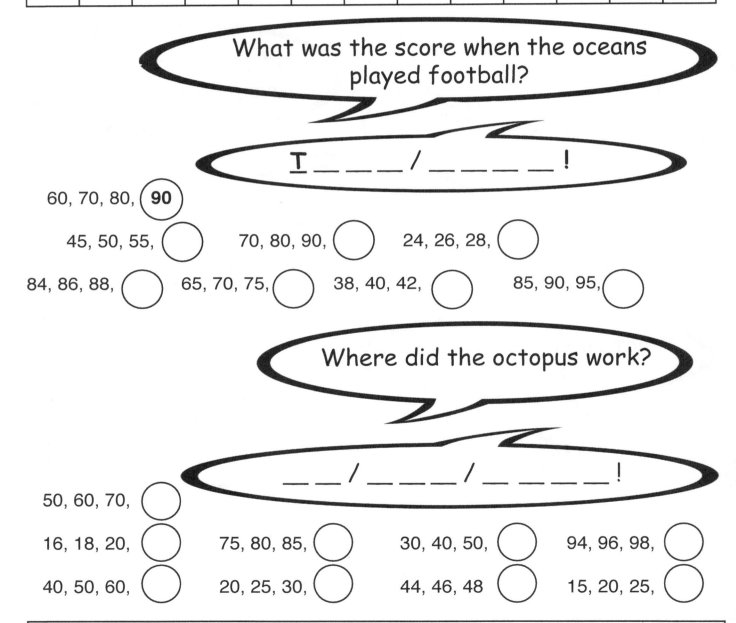

What was the score when the oceans played football?

T _ _ _ _ _ / _ _ _ _ _ !

60, 70, 80, (**90**)

45, 50, 55, ◯   70, 80, 90, ◯   24, 26, 28, ◯

84, 86, 88, ◯   65, 70, 75, ◯   38, 40, 42, ◯   85, 90, 95, ◯

Where did the octopus work?

_ _ / _ _ _ / _ _ _ _ !

50, 60, 70, ◯

16, 18, 20, ◯   75, 80, 85, ◯   30, 40, 50, ◯   94, 96, 98, ◯

40, 50, 60, ◯   20, 25, 30, ◯   44, 46, 48 ◯   15, 20, 25, ◯

Year 1 – Number and place value
*   *Count, read and write numbers to 100 in numerals; count in multiples of twos, fives and tens.*

One more or one less (1)

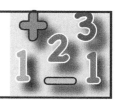

Learning objectives
I can find one more than a number.
I can find one less than a number.

To solve the jokes, answer each question and write the answer in the circle. Then use the grid to find the letter that goes with each answer and write it on the line. The first one is done for you!

29	69	9	73	20	35	48	38	59	100
C	L	U	D	A	I	B	O	E	T

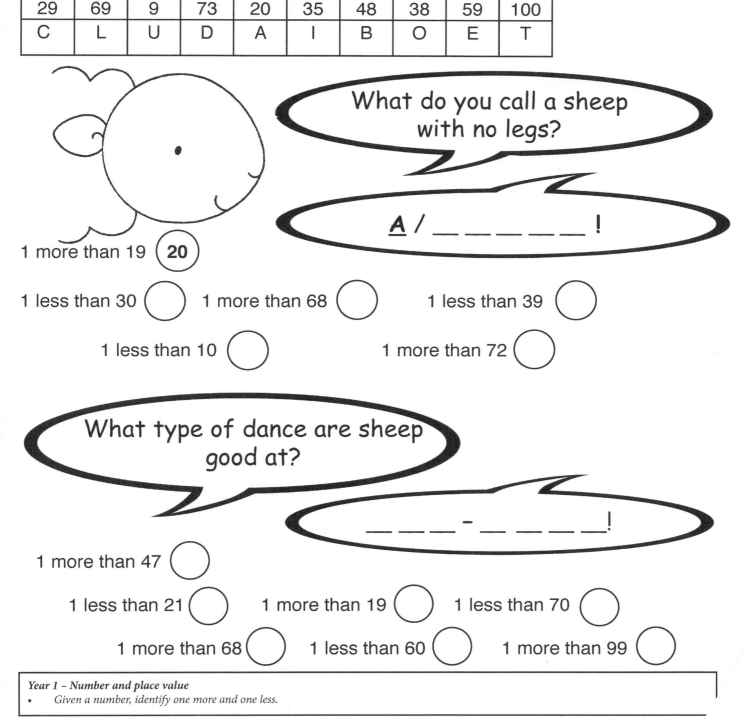

What do you call a sheep with no legs?

A / _ _ _ _ _ _ !

1 more than 19 (**20**)

1 less than 30 ◯   1 more than 68 ◯   1 less than 39 ◯

1 less than 10 ◯   1 more than 72 ◯

What type of dance are sheep good at?

_ _ _ _ - _ _ _ _ !

1 more than 47 ◯

1 less than 21 ◯   1 more than 19 ◯   1 less than 70 ◯

1 more than 68 ◯   1 less than 60 ◯   1 more than 99 ◯

Year 1 – Number and place value
• *Given a number, identify one more and one less.*

One more or one less (2)

Learning objectives
I can find one more than a number.
I can find one less than a number.

To solve the jokes, answer each question and write the answer in the circle. Then use the grid to find the letter that goes with each answer and write it on the line. The first one is done for you!

35	69	50	17	99	27	19	34	28	80
T	R	A	O	S	C	N	K	E	U

What do you call a crazy spaceman?

A _ _ / _ _ _ _ _ _ - _ _ _ _ !

1 less than 51 (**50**)   1 more than 18 ◯   1 more than 49 ◯

1 more than 98 ◯   1 less than 36 ◯   1 less than 70 ◯

1 less than 18 ◯   1 less than 20 ◯   1 more than 79 ◯

1 more than 34 ◯

What are celebrities called in space?

_ _ _ _ _ _ !

1 less than 100 ◯

1 less than 36 ◯

1 more than 49 ◯

1 more than 68 ◯   1 more than 98 ◯

Year 1 – Number and place value
• *Given a number, identify one more and one less.*

One more or one less (3)

Learning objectives
I can find one more than a number.
I can find one less than a number.

To solve the jokes, answer each question and write the answer in the circle. Then use the grid to find the letter that goes with each answer and write it on the line. The first one is done for you!

100	34	19	80	30	20	25	75	69	10
R	U	G	T	Y	S	O	A	H	L

What time did the man go to the dentist?

T _ _ _ _ _ / _ _ _ _ _ !

1 less than 81 (**80**)   1 more than 24 ( )   1 less than 26 ( )   1 more than 79 ( )

1 less than 70 ( )   1 more than 68 ( )   1 more than 33 ( )   1 more than 99 ( )

1 less than 81 ( )   1 more than 29 ( )

If a red house is made out of red bricks and a blue house is made out of blue bricks, what is a green house made out of?

1 less than 20 ( )

_ _ _ _ _ _ !

1 more than 9 ( )   1 less than 76 ( )   1 more than 19 ( )   1 less than 21 ( )

Year 1 – Number and place value
• Given a number, identify one more and one less.

Reading numbers (1)

Learning objectives
I can read and understand a number from 1 to 20 written in words.
I can write numbers from 1 to 20 in words.

To solve the joke, read the words and write each one as a number. Write the answer in the circle, then use the grid to find the letter that goes with each answer and write it on the line. The first one is done for you!

13	11	5	17	6	9	19	8	12
G	C	H	A	T	L	S	I	W

What kind of witch is most useful in the dark?

A /
_ _ _ _ _ _ _ - _ _ _ _ _ !

seventeen (17)

nine ( )   eight ( )   thirteen ( )   five ( )   six ( )   nineteen ( ) –

twelve ( )   eight ( )   six ( )   eleven ( )   five ( )

Year 1 – Number and place value
• *Read and write numbers from 1 to 20 in numerals and words.*

Reading numbers (2)

Learning objectives
I can read and understand a number from 1 to 20 written in words.
I can write numbers from 1 to 20 in words.

To solve the joke, read the words and write each one as a number. Write the answer in the circle, then use the grid to find the letter that goes with each answer and write it on the line. The first one is done for you!

12	17	2	20	10	9
C	L	E	N	T	A

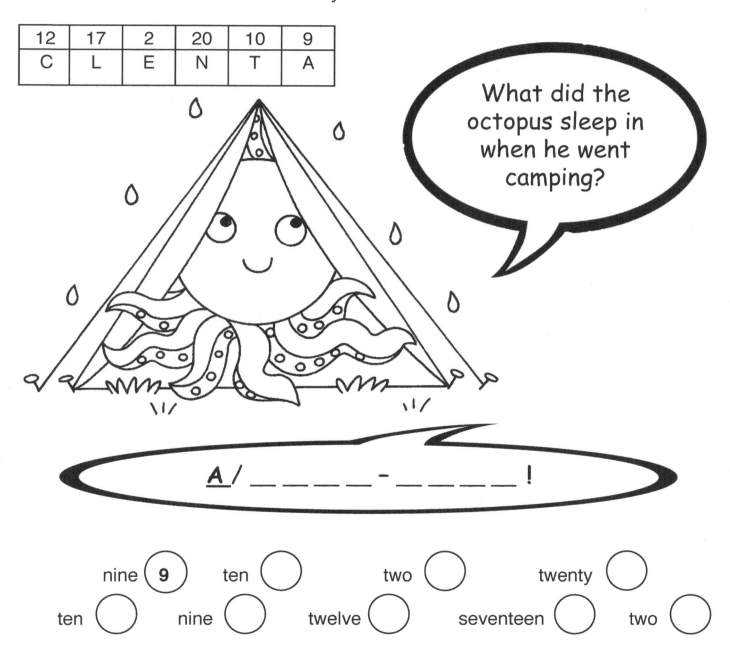

Year 1 – Number and place value
• *Read and write numbers from 1 to 20 in numerals and words.*

Reading numbers (3)

Learning objectives
I can read and understand a number from 1 to 20 written in words.
I can write numbers from 1 to 20 in words.

To solve the joke, read the words and write each one as a number. Write the answer in the circle, then use the grid to find the letter that goes with each answer and write it on the line. The first one is done for you!

1	12	3	14	5	16	7	18
F	O	L	N	A	E	T	W

How do insects count?

O _ _ _ / _ _ _ _ /
_ _ _ _ _ !

twelve (12)   fourteen ( )   sixteen ( )

seven ( )   eighteen ( )   twelve ( )

one ( )   three ( )   sixteen ( )   five ( )

Year 1 – Number and place value
•   *Read and write numbers from 1 to 20 in numerals and words.*

Writing numbers (1)

Learning objectives
I can read and understand a number from 1 to 20 written in words.
I can write numbers from 1 to 20 in words.

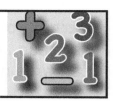

This time, write the numbers as words on the dotted lines. Then match the answer to the grid to solve the joke. The first one is done for you!

fourteen	seven	sixteen	one	twenty	eighteen	four	three
I	G	O	H	D	T	F	R

What do witches
say when they go to bed?

G _ _ _ _ / _ _ _ _ _ _ _ !

7 **s e v e n**   16 _ _ _ _ _ _ _   16 _ _ _ _ _ _ _

20 _ _ _ _ _ _   4 _ _ _ _   3 _ _ _ _ _

14 _ _ _ _ _ _ _ _   7 _ _ _ _ _   1 _ _ _

18 _ _ _ _ _ _ _ _

Year 1 – Number and place value
•   *Read and write numbers from 1 to 20 in numerals and words.*

Writing numbers (2)

Learning objectives
I can read and understand a number from 1 to 20 written in words.
I can write numbers from 1 to 20 in words.

This time, write the numbers as words on the dotted line. Then match the answer to the grid to solve the joke. The first one is done for you!

seven	fifteen	thirteen	three	eleven	five	sixteen
P	D	U	O	S	C	T

Who helped the octopus when he was feeling ill?

D _ _ _ /

_ _ _ _ _ _ !

15 **f i f t e e n**   3 _ _ _ _ _   5 _ _ _ _

16 _ _ _ _ _ _ _   3 _ _ _ _ _   7 _ _ _ _ _

13 _ _ _ _ _ _ _ _   11 _ _ _ _ _ _

Year 1 – Number and place value
- *Read and write numbers from 1 to 20 in numerals and words.*

Writing numbers (3)

This time, write the numbers as words on the dotted line. Then match the answer to the grid to solve the joke. The first one is done for you!

eleven	nine	nineteen	eight
B	Z	Y	U

How do bees like to travel?

<u>B</u> _ _ / _ _ _ _ _ _ !

11 **e l e v e n**   19 _ _ _ _ _ _ _ _

11 _ _ _ _ _ _   8 _ _ _ _ _   9 _ _ _ _

9 _ _ _ _

Year 1 – Number and place value
- *Read and write numerals from 1 to 20 in numbers and words.*

+ and − bonds to 20 (1)

Learning objectives
I know number bonds to 10.
I know number bonds to 20.

To solve the jokes, work out the answer to each question and write it in the circle. Then use the grid to find the letter that goes with each answer and write it on the line. The first one is done for you!

1	13	2	3	11	6	15	8	17	9	12
W	E	A	R	C	I	B	O	N	H	L

What has four legs but can't walk?

<u>A</u> / _ _ _ _ _ _ !

10 − 8 = (2)

20 − 9 = ( )   6 + 3 = ( )   18 + ( ) = 20   10 − 4 = ( )

10 − 7 = ( )

What gets bigger when you take more away from it?

_ / _ _ _ _ _ !

20 − 18 = ( )

20 − 11 = ( )   12 + ( ) = 20   20 − 8 = ( )   7 + ( ) = 20

Year 1 – Addition and subtraction
* *Represent and use number bonds and related subtraction facts within 20.*

+ and – bonds to 20 (2)

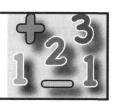

Learning objectives
I know number bonds to 10.
I know number bonds to 20.

To solve the jokes, work out the answer to each question and write it in the circle. Then use the grid to find the letter that goes with each answer and write it on the line. The first one is done for you!

12	7	16	18	4	13	9	1	15	5	20
U	S	R	T	A	A	F	B	H	I	O	M

What chocolate bar do aliens eat?

<u>M</u> _ _ _ _ / _ _ _ _ _!

10 + 10 = (**20**)   6 + ( ) = 10   20 – 4 = ( )   10 – 3 = ( )

1 + ( ) = 10   ( ) + 16 = 20   4 + ( ) = 20   ( ) + 13 = 20

What do you call a fish in outer space?

_ _ _ _ _ - _ _ _ _ _!

( ) + 3 = 10   2 + ( ) = 20   20 – ( ) = 16   ( ) + 4 = 20 –

( ) + 7 = 20   5 + ( ) = 20   20 – ( ) = 13   ( ) + 19 = 20

Year 1 – Addition and subtraction
•   *Represent and use number bonds and related subtraction facts within 20.*

+ and – bonds to 20 (3)

Learning objectives
I know number bonds to 10.
I know number bonds to 20.

To solve the jokes, work out the answer to each question and write it in the circle. Then use the grid to find the letter that goes with each answer and write it on the line. The first one is done for you!

19	18	4	17	6	12	1	10	0	3
E	F	R	I	H	H	L	O	A	T

What invention allows you to walk through walls?

T _ _ _ / _ _ _ _ _ !

$\boxed{3}$ + 7 = 10   4 + ◯ = 10   20 − 1 = ◯

10 + ◯ = 10   19 + ◯ = 20   20 − 19 = ◯   16 + ◯ = 20

What's a quick way to double your money?

_ _ _ _ _ / _ _ _ !

◯ + 2 = 20   9 + ◯ = 10   20 − 8 = ◯   20 − ◯ = 20

3 + ◯ = 20   17 + ◯ = 20

Year 1 – Addition and subtraction
• *Represent and use number bonds and related subtraction facts within 20.*

+ and – within 20 (1)

Learning objectives
I can add and subtract any two numbers up to 20.
I know what happens if I add or subtract zero.

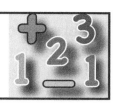

To solve the jokes, work out the answer to each question and write it in the circle. Then use the grid to find the letter that goes with each answer and write it on the line. The first one is done for you!

3	16	7	13	6	19	8	12	14	9
A	G	R	S	L	O	M	F	D	T

What goes up and down hills, through cities and towns but never moves?

A / _ _ _ _ _ !

17 – 14 = (3)

11 – 4 = ◯   12 + 7 = ◯   19 – 16 = ◯   6 + 8 = ◯

What's flies all day but never goes anywhere?

_ / _ _ _ _ _ !

12 – 9 = ◯

19 – 7 = ◯   13 – 7 = ◯   3 – 0 = ◯   9 + 7 = ◯

Year 1 – Addition and subtraction
• *Add and subtract one-digit and two-digit numbers to 20, including zero.*

+ and − within 20 (2)

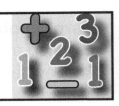

Learning objectives
I can add and subtract any two numbers up to 20.
I know what happens if I add or subtract zero.

To solve the jokes, work out the answer to each question and write it in the circle. Then use the grid to find the letter that goes with each answer and write it on the line. The first one is done for you!

17	6	13	19	9	18	15	11	16	7	20
Y	M	K	S	O	T	R	U	E	N	A

Where do cows go on holiday?

M _ _ _ / _ _ _ _ _ _ !

14 − 8 = (6)   17 − 8 = ( )   4 + 5 = ( )

9 + 8 = ( )   15 − 6 = ( )   10 + 5 = ( )   5 + 8 = ( )

Where do cows go to learn about the past?

_ _ / _ _ _ _ - _ _ _ _ _ !

20 + 0 = ( )

11 − 5 = ( )   9 − 0 = ( )   6 + 3 = ( )

11 + 8 = ( )   8 + 8 = ( )   17 − 6 = ( )   15 − 9 = ( )

Year 1 – Addition and subtraction
• *Add and subtract one-digit and two-digit numbers to 20, including zero.*

+ and – within 20 (3)

To solve the jokes, work out the answer to each question and write it in the circle. Then use the grid to find the letter that goes with each answer and write it on the line. The first one is done for you!

18	10	7	3	14	11	5	8	13	16	9
T	B	H	S	U	R	E	C	N	A	P

What is an astronaut's favourite part of a computer?

T _ _ / _ _ _ _ _ _ / _ _ _ !

15 + 3 = (18)   12 – 5 = ◯   20 – 15 = ◯   11 – 8 = ◯

2 + 7 = ◯   19 – 3 = ◯   8 – 0 = ◯   3 + 2 = ◯

14 – 4 = ◯   9 + 7 = ◯   17 – 6 = ◯

What kind of songs do the planets sing?

_ _ _ / _ _ _ _ _ !

13 + 0 = ◯   11 – 6 = ◯   19 – 10 = ◯

9 + 9 = ◯   8 + 6 = ◯   19 – 6 = ◯   12 – 7 = ◯   19 – 16 = ◯

Year 1 – Addition and subtraction
• *Add and subtract one-digit and two-digit numbers to 20, including zero.*

Simple multiplication and division (1)

Learning objectives
I can use repeated addition, pictures or arrays to help me
  multiply two numbers.
I can use grouping or sharing to help me divide numbers.

*To solve the joke, work out the answer to each question and write it in the circle.
Then use the grid to find the letter that goes with each answer and write it on the
line. The first one is done for you!*

2	4	9	3	16	5	10	6	15	1	14	8
A	E	H	P	O	G	R	S	K	T	C	I

What did the pig wear
around his neck?

How many groups
of 2 are
in 4? **2**

<u>A</u> / _ _ _ _ _ / _ _ _ !

What is 6 shared
between 2?

What is
double 4?

What is half
of 10?

What is 2
groups of 3?

What is a
quarter of 4?

What is 4
lots of 2?

How many groups
of 2 are in 8?

Year 1 – Multiplication and division
* *Solve one-step problems involving multiplication and division, by calculating the answer using concrete objects, pictorial representations
  and arrays with the support of the teacher.*

Simple multiplication and division (2)

To solve the joke, work out the answer to each question and write it in the circle. Then use the grid to find the letter that goes with each answer and write it on the line. The first one is done for you!

2	4	9	3	16	5	10	6	15	1	14	8
A	E	H	P	O	G	R	S	K	T	C	I

What karate moves do pigs do?

P _ _ _ / _ _ _ _ !

What is half of 6? **3**

What is double 8? ◯

What is 5 groups of 2 ◯

What is 3 lots of 5? ◯

What is double 7? ◯

What is 3 groups of 3? ◯

What is 8 lots of 2? ◯

What is 9 shared between 3? ◯

Year 1 – Multiplication and division
- *Solve one-step problems involving multiplication and division, by calculating the answer using concrete objects, pictorial representations and arrays with the support of the teacher.*

Simple multiplication and division (3)

*To solve the joke, work out the answer to each question and write it in the circle.
Then use the grid to find the letter that goes with each answer and write it on the
line. The first one is done for you!*

7	2	8	1	20	3	10	4	12	5	14	21
D	A	C	I	B	T	H	L	R	U	N	E

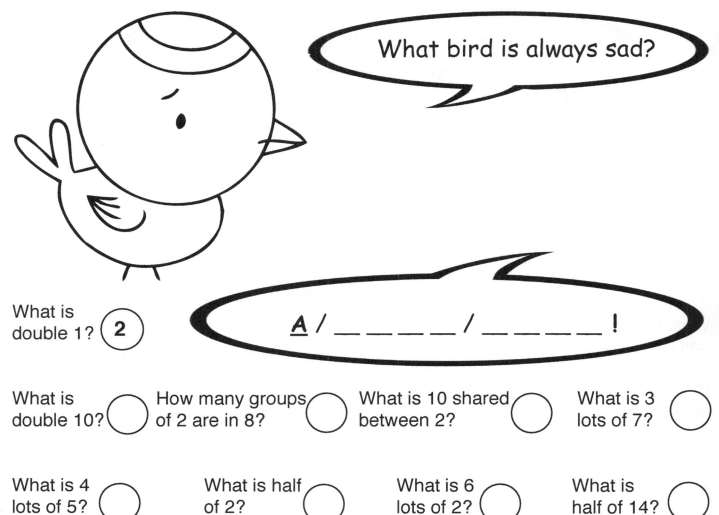

What bird is always sad?

What is double 1? (**2**)

A / _ _ _ _ _ / _ _ _ _ _ !

What is double 10? ◯

How many groups of 2 are in 8? ◯

What is 10 shared between 2? ◯

What is 3 lots of 7? ◯

What is 4 lots of 5? ◯

What is half of 2? ◯

What is 6 lots of 2? ◯

What is half of 14? ◯

Simple multiplication and division (4)

Learning objectives
I can use repeated addition, pictures or arrays to help me multiply two numbers.
I can use grouping or sharing to help me divide numbers.

To solve the joke, work out the answer to each question and write it in the circle. Then use the grid to find the letter that goes with each answer and write it on the line. The first one is done for you!

7	2	8	1	20	3	10	4	12	5	14	6
D	A	C	I	B	T	H	L	R	U	N	E

What bird can carry the most weight?

What is half of 6? (3)

T _ _ / _ _ _ _ _ _ !

What is 2 lots of 5? ◯

What is double 3? ◯

What is 4 groups of 2? ◯

What is double 6? ◯

What is a quarter of 8? ◯

What is 7 lots of 2? ◯

What is half of 12? ◯

Year 1 – Multiplication and division
* *Solve one-step problems involving multiplication and division, by calculating the answer using concrete objects, pictorial representations and arrays with the support of the teacher.*

Simple multiplication and division (5)

Learning objectives
I can use repeated addition, pictures or arrays to help me multiply
two numbers.
I can use grouping or sharing to help me divide numbers.

*To solve the joke, work out the answer to each question and write it in the circle.
Then use the grid to find the letter that goes with each answer and write it on the
line. The first one is done for you!*

1	8	2	20	4	14	5	12	6	10	18
A	G	E	T	N	Y	U	W	R	I	K

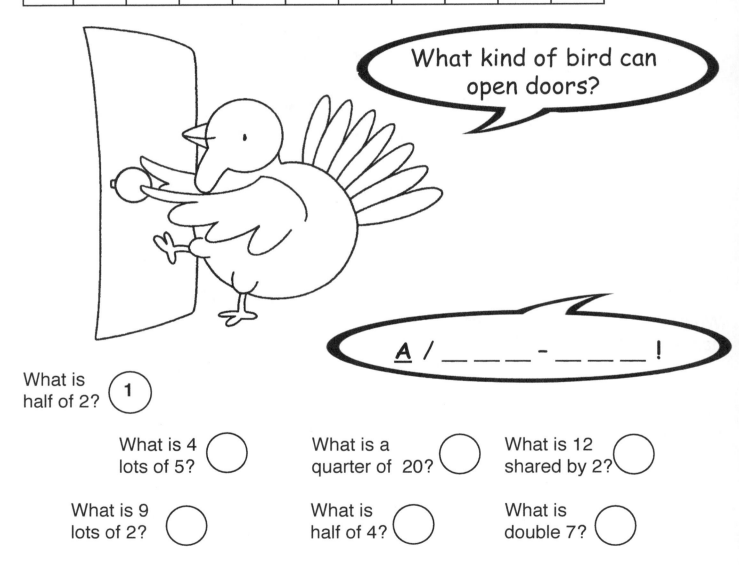

What is
half of 2? (1)

What kind of bird can
open doors?

A / _ _ _ _ - _ _ _ _ !

What is 4
lots of 5? ( )

What is a
quarter of 20? ( )

What is 12
shared by 2? ( )

What is 9
lots of 2? ( )

What is
half of 4? ( )

What is
double 7? ( )

Year 1 – Multiplication and division
- *Solve one-step problems involving multiplication and division, by calculating the answer using concrete objects, pictorial representations and arrays with the support of the teacher.*

Simple multiplication and division (6)

Learning objectives

I can use repeated addition, pictures or arrays to help me multiply two numbers.

I can use grouping or sharing to help me divide numbers.

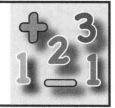

To solve the joke, work out the answer to each question and write it in the circle. Then use the grid to find the letter that goes with each answer and write it on the line. The first one is done for you!

1	8	2	20	4	14	5	12	6	10	18
A	G	E	T	N	Y	U	W	R	I	K

What noise does a bird's telephone make?

What is double 6? (12)

W _ _ _ _ / _ _ _ _ _ !

What is 2 groups of 5? ◯

How many groups of 2 are in 8? ◯

What is double 4? ◯

What is 3 lots of 4? ◯

What is double 5? ◯

What is 4 lots of 1? ◯

What is 4 groups of 2? ◯

Year 1 – Multiplication and division
- *Solve one-step problems involving multiplication and division, by calculating the answer using concrete objects, pictorial representations and arrays with the support of the teacher.*

Counting forwards and backwards in steps of 2, 3, 5 and 10 (1)

Learning objectives
I can count forwards and backwards in 2s, 3s and 5s.
I can count forwards and backwards in 10s starting at any number.

To solve the joke, work out the number that comes next and write it in the circle. Then use the grid to find the letter that goes with each answer and write it on the line. The first one is done for you!

81	53	12	36	80	24	90	45	102	60	105	100	8
P	K	L	Y	I	U	A	M	E	O	H	S	D

What do you get if you cross a cow with a camel?

L __ __ __ __ / __ __ __ __ - __ __ __ __ !

6, 8, 10, (12)   15, 18, 21, ◯   30, 35, 40, ◯

51, 61, 71, ◯   42, 40, 38, ◯

36, 39, 42, ◯   95, 90, 85, ◯   21, 18, 15, ◯   83, 73, 63, ◯ –

94, 96, 98, ◯   75, 85, 95, ◯   99, 96, 93, ◯

23, 33, 43, ◯   93, 96, 99, ◯

Year 2 – Number and place value
• *Count in steps of 2, 3, and 5 from 0, and in tens from any number, forward and backward.*

Counting forwards and backwards in steps of 2, 3, 5 and 10 (2)

Learning objectives
I can count forwards and backwards in 2s, 3s and 5s.
I can count forwards and backwards in 10s starting at any number.

To solve the joke, work out the number that comes next and write it in the circle. Then use the grid to find the letter that goes with each answer and write it on the line. The first one is done for you!

81	53	12	36	80	24	90	45	102	60	105	100	8
P	K	L	Y	I	U	A	M	E	O	H	S	D

Year 2 – Number and place value
• Count in steps of 2, 3, and 5 from 0, and in tens from any number, forward and backward.

Counting forwards and backwards in steps of 2, 3, 5 and 10 (3)

Learning objectives
I can count forwards and backwards in 2s, 3s and 5s.
I can count forwards and backwards in 10s starting at any number.

To solve the joke, work out the number that comes next and write it in the circle. Then use the grid to find the letter that goes with each answer and write it on the line. The first one is done for you!

86	45	72	51	63	42	95	30	28	100	18	78
O	N	L	E	A	S	Z	P	Y	R	B	I

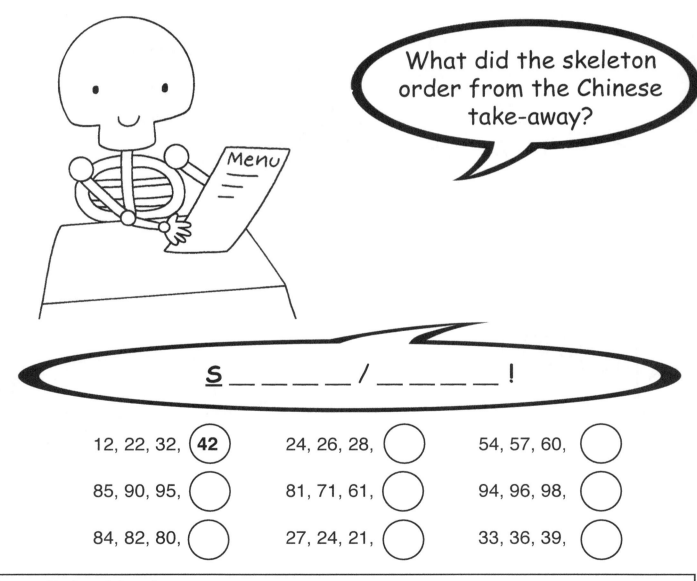

What did the skeleton order from the Chinese take-away?

S _ _ _ _ _ / _ _ _ _ _ !

12, 22, 32, (42)　　24, 26, 28, ◯　　54, 57, 60, ◯

85, 90, 95, ◯　　81, 71, 61, ◯　　94, 96, 98, ◯

84, 82, 80, ◯　　27, 24, 21, ◯　　33, 36, 39, ◯

Year 2 – Number and place value
* *Count in steps of 2, 3, and 5 from 0, and in tens from any number, forward and backward.*

Counting forwards and backwards in steps of 2, 3, 5 and 10 (4)

Learning objectives
I can count forwards and backwards in 2s, 3s and 5s.
I can count forwards and backwards in 10s starting at any number.

To solve the joke, work out the number that comes next and write it in the circle. Then use the grid to find the letter that goes with each answer and write it on the line. The first one is done for you!

86	45	72	51	63	42	95	30	28	100	18	78
O	N	L	E	A	S	Z	P	Y	R	B	I

What do you call a skeleton that won't get out of bed?

L _ _ _ _ - _ _ _ _ _ !

63, 66, 69, (72)   33, 43, 53, ◯   110, 105, 100, ◯   34, 32, 30, ◯ –

9, 12, 15, ◯   92, 90, 88, ◯   60, 55, 50, ◯

42, 45, 48, ◯   72, 62, 52, ◯

Counting forwards and backwards in steps of 2, 3, 5 and 10 (5)

Learning objectives

I can count forwards and backwards in 2s, 3s and 5s.

I can count forwards and backwards in 10s starting at any number.

To solve the joke, work out the number that comes next and write it in the circle. Then use the grid to find the letter that goes with each answer and write it on the line. The first one is done for you!

18	92	30	75	50	13	0	100	63	1	45
O	A	P	T	U	K	S	I	N	Y	B

What do you call a cat wearing shoes?

P̲ _ _ _ _ / _ _ _ / _ _ _ _ _ _ !

15, 20, 25, (**30**)   44, 46, 48, ◯   30, 20, 10, ◯

9, 6, 3, ◯   70, 80, 90, ◯   54, 57, 60, ◯

30, 35, 40, ◯   24, 22, 20, ◯   9, 12, 15, ◯

105, 95, 85, ◯   6, 4, 2, ◯

Year 2 – Number and place value
- *Count in steps of 2, 3, and 5 from 0, and in tens from any number, forward and backward.*

Counting forwards and backwards in steps of 2, 3, 5 and 10 (6)

Learning objectives
I can count forwards and backwards in 2s, 3s and 5s.
I can count forwards and backwards in 10s starting at any number.

To solve the joke, work out the number that comes next and write it in the circle. Then use the grid to find the letter that goes with each answer and write it on the line. The first one is done for you!

18	92	30	75	50	13	0	100	63	1	45
O	A	P	T	U	K	S	I	N	Y	B

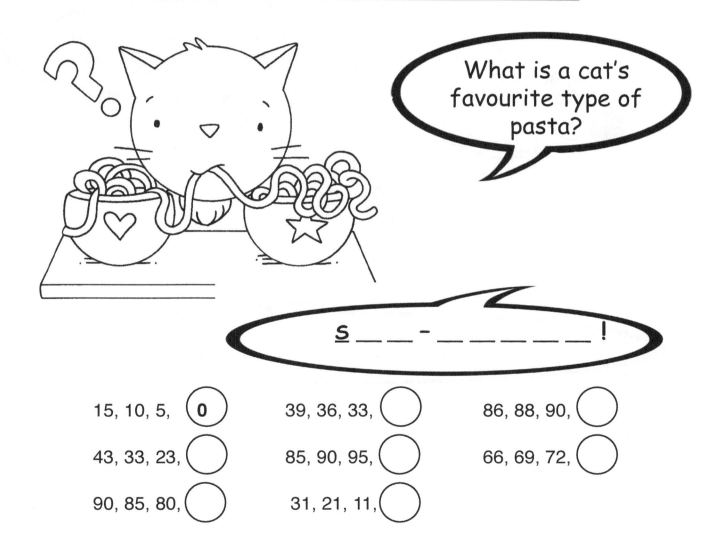

What is a cat's favourite type of pasta?

s_ _ _ - _ _ _ _ _ _ !

15, 10, 5, ⓪   39, 36, 33, ◯   86, 88, 90, ◯

43, 33, 23, ◯   85, 90, 95, ◯   66, 69, 72, ◯

90, 85, 80, ◯   31, 21, 11, ◯

Year 2 – Number and place value
• *Count in steps of 2, 3, and 5 from 0, and in tens from any number, forward and backward.*

Place value tens and ones (1)

Learning objectives
I know the value of each digit in numbers up to 100.

To solve the joke, use place value to work out the value of the underlined digits and write the answer in the circle. Then use the grid to find the letter that goes with each answer and write it on the line. The first one is done for you!

1	2	3	4	5	6	7	8	9	10	20	30	40	50	60	70	80	90
C	N	L	Y	R	E	H	Z	U	T	P	O	B	A	S	K	J	I

What do frogs like to drink on hot days?

<u>C</u> _ _ _ _ _ – _ – _ _ _ _ !

4<u>1</u> (1)   2<u>5</u> ( )   <u>3</u>6 ( )   <u>5</u>9 ( )   <u>7</u>7 ( ) – <u>5</u>4 ( ) –

2<u>1</u> ( )   <u>3</u>8 ( )   4<u>3</u> ( )   <u>5</u>6 ( )

Year 2 – Number and place value
* *Recognise the place value of each digit in a two-digit number (tens, ones).*

Place value tens and ones (2)

Learning objectives
I know the value of each digit in numbers up to 100.

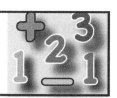

To solve the joke, use place value to work out the value of the underlined digits and write the answer in the circle. Then use the grid to find the letter that goes with each answer and write it on the line. The first one is done for you!

1	2	3	4	5	6	7	8	9	10	20	30	40	50	60	70	80	90
C	N	L	Y	R	E	H	Z	U	T	P	O	B	A	S	K	J	I

What do you get if you cross a bumblebee with a rabbit?

_A_ / _ _ _ _ _ _ _ / _ _ _ _ _ _ !

5<u>9</u> (50)   2<u>7</u> ( )   <u>3</u>6 ( )   5<u>2</u> ( )   4<u>6</u> ( )   7<u>4</u> ( )

<u>4</u>8 ( )   8<u>9</u> ( )   4<u>2</u> ( )   7<u>2</u> ( )   9<u>4</u> ( )

Year 2 – Number and place value
• *Recognise the place value of each digit in a two-digit number (tens, ones).*

Place value tens and ones (3)

Learning objectives
I know the value of each digit in numbers up to 100.

To solve the joke, use place value to work out the value of the underlined digits and write the answer in the circle. Then use the grid to find the letter that goes with each answer and write it on the line. The first one is done for you!

1	2	3	4	5	6	7	8	9	10	20	30	40	50	60	70	80	90
N	C	A	K	R	T	P	I	Y	M	E	O	L	U	W	Q	D	S

What do you call a 90 year old ant?

A _ / _ _ _ - _ _ _ _ !

2<u>3</u> (3)   5<u>1</u> ( )

3<u>3</u> ( )   7<u>1</u> ( )   4<u>6</u> ( ) – 6<u>8</u> ( )   <u>7</u>9 ( )   <u>5</u>4 ( )   2<u>1</u> ( )

Year 2 – Number and place value
• *Recognise the place value of each digit in a two-digit number (tens, ones).*

Place value tens and ones (4)

Learning objectives
I know the value of each digit in numbers up to 100.

To solve the joke, use place value to work out the value of the underlined digits and write the answer in the circle. Then use the grid to find the letter that goes with each answer and write it on the line. The first one is done for you!

1	2	3	4	5	6	7	8	9	10	20	30	40	50	60	70	80	90
N	C	A	K	R	T	P	I	Y	M	E	O	L	U	W	Q	D	S

What do you call a cockerel that wakes you up at the same time every morning?

A __ / _ _ _ _ _ _ / _ _ _ _ _ _ !

5**3** (3)　　9**1** ( )

43 ( )　　**4**5 ( )　　6**3** ( )　　4**5** ( )　　**1**7 ( )

7**2** ( )　　**4**1 ( )　　**5**2 ( )　　9**2** ( )　　6**4** ( )

Year 2 – Number and place value
- *Recognise the place value of each digit in a two-digit number (tens, ones).*

Place value tens and ones (5)

Learning objectives
I know the value of each digit in numbers up to 100.

To solve the jokes, use place value to work out the value of the underlined digits and write the answer in the circle. Then use the grid to find the letter that goes with each answer and write it on the line. The first one is done for you!

1	2	3	4	5	6	7	8	9	10	20	30	40	50	60	70	80	90
C	M	B	L	E	N	O	T	P	G	V	H	R	K	I	A	F	S

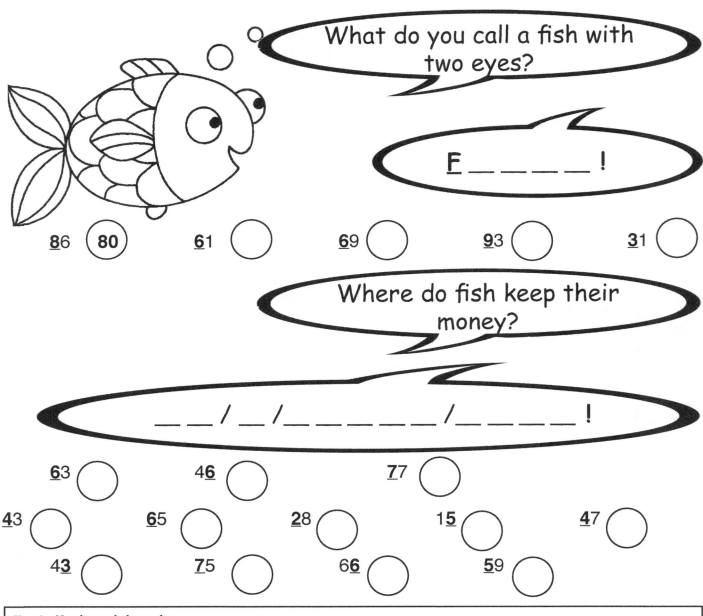

What do you call a fish with two eyes?

<u>F</u> _ _ _ _ _ !

<u>8</u>6 (80)   <u>6</u>1 ◯   <u>6</u>9 ◯   <u>9</u>3 ◯   <u>3</u>1 ◯

Where do fish keep their money?

_ _ / _ _ / _ _ _ _ _ / _ _ _ _ !

<u>6</u>3 ◯   4<u>6</u> ◯   <u>7</u>7 ◯

4<u>3</u> ◯   <u>6</u>5 ◯   <u>2</u>8 ◯   1<u>5</u> ◯   <u>4</u>7 ◯

4<u>3</u> ◯   <u>7</u>5 ◯   66 ◯   <u>5</u>9 ◯

Year 2 – Number and place value
• *Recognise the place value of each digit in a two-digit number (tens, ones).*

Reading numbers to 100 (1)

Learning objectives
I can read and understand a number from 1 to 100 written in words.
I can write numbers from 1 to 100 in words.

To solve the joke, read the words and write each one as a number. Write the answer in the circle, then use the grid to find the letter that goes with each answer and write it on the line. The first one is done for you!

22	37	50	17	64	60	46	73
A	P	B	R	T	S	F	L

What did the vampire use to get in and out of his house at night?

<u>A</u> / _ _ _ _ / _ _ _ _ !

twenty-two (22)

fifty ( )   twenty-two ( )   sixty-four ( )

forty-six ( )   seventy-three ( )   twenty-two ( )   thirty-seven ( )

Year 2 – Number and place value
• *Read and write numbers to at least 100 in numerals and in words.*

Reading numbers to 100 (2)

Learning objectives
I can read and understand a number from 1 to 100 written in words.
I can write numbers from 1 to 100 in words.

To solve the joke, read the words and write each one as a number. Write the answer in the circle, then use the grid to find the letter that goes with each answer and write it on the line. The first one is done for you!

83	100	18	65	31	13	56	87	38
A	O	R	W	I	S	N	T	B

What bow can't be tied?

<u>A</u> / _ _ _ _ _ _ _ _ !

eighty-three (83)

eighteen ( )   eighty-three ( )   thirty-one ( )   fifty-six ( )

thirty-eight ( )   one hundred ( )   sixty-five ( )

Year 2 – Number and place value
• *Read and write numbers to at least 100 in numerals and in words.*

Reading numbers to 100 (3)

Learning objectives
I can read and understand a number from 1 to 100 written in words.
I can write numbers from 1 to 100 in words.

To solve the joke, read the words and write each one as a number. Write the answer in the circle, then use the grid to find the letter that goes with each answer and write it on the line. The first one is done for you!

80	38	27	69	83	96	72	18
K	A	I	N	M	E	O	S

What do you call a cow at the North Pole?

A _ /

_ _ _ _ _ _ - _ _ _ _ !

thirty-eight (**38**)   sixty-nine ◯

ninety-six ◯   eighteen ◯   eighty ◯   twenty-seven ◯

eighty-three ◯   seventy-two ◯   seventy-two ◯

Year 2 – Number and place value
• *Read and write numbers to at least 100 in numerals and in words.*

Writing numbers to 100 (1)

Learning objectives
I can read and understand a number from 1 to 100 written in words.
I can write numbers from 1 to 100 in words.

To solve the joke, write the numbers as words inside the oval shape, then use the grid to find the letter that goes with each answer and write it on the line. The first one is done for you!

fifty-eight	ninety-one	eighty-five	ninety-two	sixty-two	nineteen	one hundred
M	F	I	A	L	N	G

What type of post did the celebrity vampire get?

F _ _ _ _ / _ _ _ _ !

91 — ninety-one

92

19

100

58

92

85

62

Year 2 – Number and place value
• Read and write numbers to at least 100 in numerals and in words.

Writing numbers to 100 (2)

Learning objectives
I can read and understand a number from 1 to 100 written in words.
I can write numbers from 1 to 100 in words.

To solve the joke, write the numbers as words inside the oval shape, then use the grid to find the letter that goes with each answer and write it on the line. The first one is done for you!

seventy-four	twenty-one	fifty-two	forty-seven	twenty-five	twelve	ninety-two
R	Y	N	O	E	U	S

Writing numbers to 100 (3)

Learning objectives
I can read and understand a number from 1 to 100 written in words.
I can write numbers from 1 to 100 in words.

To solve the joke, write the numbers as words inside the oval shape, then use the grid to find the letter that goes with each answer and write it on the line. The first one is done for you!

seventeen	twenty-five	seventy	fifty-two	sixteen	one hundred	sixty
S	A	T	C	R	O	P

Year 2 – Number and place value
• *Read and write numbers to at least 100 in numerals and in words.*

Number facts to 20 and 10s to 100 (1)

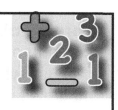

Learning objectives
I can add or subtract any two numbers up to 20.
I can use what I know about numbers up to 20 to add and subtract multiples of ten up to 100.

To solve the jokes, work out the answer to each question and write it in the circle. Then use the grid to find the letter that goes with each answer and write it on the line. The first one is done for you!

12	60	50	9	18	100	15	19	70	8	90	80
K	A	S	D	T	O	R	U	I	C	M	H

What do hedgehogs say when they hug?

<u>O</u> _ _ _ _ !

$30 + 70 =$ (**100**) $12 + 7 =$ ◯ $19 - 11 =$ ◯ $60 + 20 =$ ◯

What is the most musical part of a chicken?

_ _ / _ _ _ _ _ / _ _ _ _ _ _ !

$100 - 40 =$ ◯

$14 - 5 =$ ◯ $3 + 12 =$ ◯ $8 + 11 =$ ◯ $30 + 60 =$ ◯

$90 - 40 =$ ◯ $5 + 13 =$ ◯ $20 + 50 =$ ◯ $20 - 12 =$ ◯ $17 - 5 =$ ◯

Year 2 – Addition and subtraction
  • *Recall and use addition and subtraction facts to 20 fluently, and derive and use related facts up to 100.*

Number facts to 20 and 10s to 100 (2)

Learning objectives
I can add or subtract any two numbers up to 20.
I can use what I know about numbers up to 20 to add and subtract multiples of ten up to 100.

To solve the jokes, work out the answer to each question and write it in the circle. Then use the grid to find the letter that goes with each answer and write it on the line. The first one is done for you!

15	5	20	30	8	70	7	90	19
L	P	I	W	E	B	A	S	T

Where do wasps go when they are ill?

W _ _ _ _ - _ _ _ _ _ !

70 − 40 = (**30**)   15 − 8 = ◯   50 + 40 = ◯   11 − 6 = ◯

90 − 70 = ◯   11 + 8 = ◯   12 − 5 = ◯   7 + 8 = ◯

What did the spider make on the computer?

_ / _ _ _ / _ _ _ _ !

11 − 4 = ◯

100 − 70 = ◯   20 − 12 = ◯   30 + 40 = ◯

20 + 70 = ◯   100 − 80 = ◯   14 + 5 = ◯   15 − 7 = ◯

Year 2 – Addition and subtraction
• *Recall and use addition and subtraction facts to 20 fluently, and derive and use related facts up to 100.*

Number facts to 20 and 10s to 100 (3)

Learning objectives
I can add or subtract any two numbers up to 20.
I can use what I know about numbers up to 20 to add and subtract multiples of ten up to 100.

To solve the joke, work out the answer to each question and write it in the circle. Then use the grid to find the letter that goes with each answer and write it on the line. The first one is done for you!

40	10	30	7	15	100	50	12	80	90	17
S	A	M	O	L	N	B	R	T	H	E

What did the skeleton use to ring his friends?

T _ _ / _ _ _ _ - _ _ _ _ !

50 + 30 = (80)   100 − 10 = ◯   14 + 3 = ◯

20 + 60 = ◯   20 − 3 = ◯   7 + 8 = ◯   9 + 8 = ◯ −

80 − 30 = ◯   16 − 9 = ◯   100 − 0 = ◯   11 + 6 = ◯

Year 2 – Addition and subtraction
• *Recall and use addition and subtraction facts to 20 fluently, and derive and use related facts up to 100.*

© Katherine Bennett and Brilliant Publications
This page may be copied by the purchasing institution only.

Number facts to 20 and 10s to 100 (4)

To solve the joke, work out the answer to each question and write it in the circle. Then use the grid to find the letter that goes with each answer and write it on the line. The first one is done for you!

40	10	30	7	15	100	50	12	80	90	17
S	A	M	O	L	N	B	R	T	H	E

What is a skeleton's favourite musical instrument?

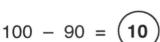

A / _ _ _ _ _ _ _ _ _ _ !

$100 - 90 =$ (**10**)

$10 + 70 =$ ◯

$5 + 7 =$ ◯

$12 - 5 =$ ◯

$90 - 60 =$ ◯

$70 - 20 =$ ◯

$19 - 12 =$ ◯

$60 + 40 =$ ◯

$7 + 10 =$ ◯

Add and subtract 2-digit and 1-digit (1)

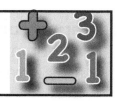

Learning objectives
I can add a two-digit number to a one-digit number.
I can subtract a one-digit number from a two-digit number.

To solve the joke, write the answer to the maths question in the circle. Then use the grid to find the letter that goes with each answer and write it on the line. The first one is done for you!

48	35	66	27	73	31	46	24	38	84	68	57	76	98
O	F	E	S	N	J	P	T	A	M	L	D	I	H

What do you call a fish who is a spy?

J _ _ _ _ _ / _ _ _ _ _ !

23 + 8 = (31)   45 − 7 = ◯   78 + 6 = ◯   75 − 9 = ◯   36 − 9 = ◯

39 + 7 = ◯   54 − 6 = ◯   66 + 7 = ◯   63 − 6 = ◯

Year 2 – Addition and subtraction
- *Add and subtract numbers using concrete objects, pictorial representations, and mentally, including:*
  - *★ a two-digit number and ones.*

Add and subtract 2-digit and 1-digit (2)

Learning objectives
I can add a two-digit number to a one-digit number.
I can subtract a one-digit number from a two-digit number.

To solve the joke, write the answer to the maths question in the circle. Then use the grid to find the letter that goes with each answer and write it on the line. The first one is done for you!

48	35	66	27	73	31	46	24	38	84	68	57	76	98
O	F	E	S	N	J	P	Y	A	M	L	D	I	H

What fish goes well with ice-cream?

<u>J</u> _ _ _ _ _ / _ _ _ _ _ !

26 + 5 = (**31**)

57 + 9 = ◯

71 − 3 = ◯

75 − 7 = ◯

16 + 8 = ◯

42 − 7 = ◯

71 + 5 = ◯

35 − 8 = ◯

89 + 9 = ◯

Year 2 – Addition and subtraction
- *Add and subtract numbers using concrete objects, pictorial representations, and mentally, including:*
  * *a two-digit number and ones.*

Add and subtract 2-digit and 1-digit (3)

Learning objectives
I can add a two-digit number to a one-digit number.
I can subtract a one-digit number from a two-digit number.

To solve the joke, write the answer to the maths question in the circle. Then use the grid to find the letter that goes with each answer and write it on the line. The first one is done for you!

29	45	68	83	18	37	56	72	91	26	75	62	34
L	E	P	G	D	H	S	K	O	T	U	I	C

What is a ghost's favourite fairy tale?

<u>G</u> _ _ _ _ _ - _ _ _ _ _ _ _ !

75 + 8 = （83）   43 − 6 = ◯   88 + 3 = ◯   83 − 8 = ◯

22 + 7 = ◯ −

23 − 5 = ◯   56 + 6 = ◯   37 − 8 = ◯   84 + 7 = ◯

43 − 9 = ◯   68 + 4 = ◯   63 − 7 = ◯

Year 2 – Addition and subtraction
- *Add and subtract numbers using concrete objects, pictorial representations, and mentally, including:*
  * *a two-digit number and ones.*

Add and subtract 2-digit and 1-digit (4)

Learning objectives
I can add a two-digit number to a one-digit number.
I can subtract a one-digit number from a two-digit number.

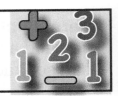

To solve the joke, write the answer to the maths question in the circle. Then use the grid to find the letter that goes with each answer and write it on the line. The first one is done for you!

29	45	68	83	18	37	56	72	91	26	75	62	34
L	E	P	G	D	H	S	K	O	T	U	I	C

What is a ghost's favourite type of pasta?

<u>S</u> _ _ _ _ _ - _ _ _ _ !

47 + 9 = (**56**)   74 – 6 = ◯   86 + 5 = ◯   93 – 2 = ◯

66 + 6 = ◯ –

52 – 7 = ◯   18 + 8 = ◯   31 – 5 = ◯   59 + 3 = ◯

Year 2 – Addition and subtraction
* *Add and subtract numbers using concrete objects, pictorial representations, and mentally, including:*
  * *a two-digit number and ones.*

Add and subtract 2-digit and 1-digit (5)

Learning objectives
I can add a two-digit number to a one-digit number.
I can subtract a one-digit number from a two-digit number.

To solve the joke, write the answer to the maths question in the circle. Then use the grid to find the letter that goes with each answer and write it on the line. The first one is done for you!

97	52	81	35	64	73	46	92	85	27	61	58
F	R	H	T	S	A	W	O	V	B	C	E

What did the sheep say to his girlfriend at the farm gate?

A _ _ _ _ _ / _ _ _ !

65 + 8 = (**73**)   92 + 5 = ◯   42 − 7 = ◯   49 + 9 = ◯

58 − 6 = ◯

52 + 6 = ◯   53 − 7 = ◯   49 + 9 = ◯

Year 2 – Addition and subtraction
* *Add and subtract numbers using concrete objects, pictorial representations, and mentally, including:*
  * *a two-digit number and ones.*

Add and subtract 2–digit and 1–digit (6)

Learning objectives
I can add a two-digit number to a one-digit number.
I can subtract a one-digit number from a two-digit number.

To solve the joke, write the answer to the maths question in the circle. Then use the grid to find the letter that goes with each answer and write it on the line. The first one is done for you!

97	52	81	35	64	73	46	92	85	27	61	58
F	R	H	T	S	A	W	O	V	B	C	E

What did one sheep say to the other when he got muddy?

<u>H</u> _ _ _ _ / _ / _ _ _ _ _ !

89 − 8 = (**81**)   67 + 6 = ◯   92 − 7 = ◯   53 + 5 = ◯

81 − 8 = ◯

19 + 8 = ◯   66 + 7 = ◯   68 + 5 = ◯   44 − 9 = ◯

75 + 6 = ◯

Year 2 – Addition and subtraction
•   *Add and subtract numbers using concrete objects, pictorial representations, and mentally, including:*
   * *a two-digit number and ones.*

Add and subtract 2–digits and a multiple of ten (1)

Learning objectives
I can add a multiple of ten to a two-digit number.
I can subtract a multiple of ten from a two-digit number.

To solve the joke, write the answer to the maths question in the circle. Then use the grid to find the letter that goes with each answer and write it on the line. The first one is done for you!

53	54	38	88	43	65	94	87	62	37	77	69
E	S	H	O	A	R	P	N	I	Y	T	M

What do you get if you wrap a snake in pastry?

<u>A</u> / _ _ _ _ – _ _ _ _ !

13 + 30 = (**43**)

34 + 60 = ◯   82 – 20 = ◯   23 + 30 = ◯   –

97 – 20 = ◯   18 + 20 = ◯   98 – 10 = ◯   17 + 70 = ◯

Year 2 – Addition and subtraction
*   *Add and subtract numbers using concrete objects, pictorial representations, and mentally, including:*
    *   *a two-digit number and tens.*

Add and subtract 2-digits and a multiple of ten (2)

Learning objectives

I can add a multiple of ten to a two-digit number.
I can subtract a multiple of ten from a two-digit number.

To solve the joke, write the answer to the maths question in the circle. Then use the grid to find the letter that goes with each answer and write it on the line. The first one is done for you!

53	54	38	88	43	65	94	87	62	37	77	69
E	S	H	O	A	R	P	N	I	Y	T	M

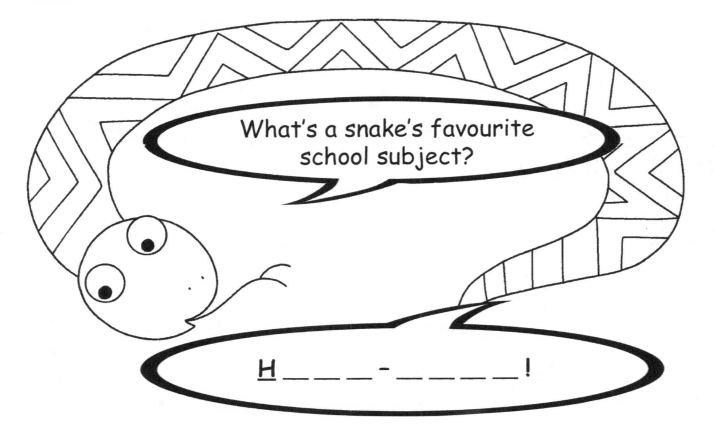

What's a snake's favourite school subject?

<u>H</u> _ _ _ - _ _ _ _ !

$68 - 30 = \boxed{38}$ $22 + 40 = \boxed{62}$ $94 - 40 = \boxed{54}$ $34 + 20 = \boxed{54}$

$47 + 30 = \boxed{77}$ $48 + 40 = \boxed{88}$ $85 - 20 = \boxed{65}$ $17 + 20 = \boxed{37}$

Year 2 – Addition and subtraction
- *Add and subtract numbers using concrete objects, pictorial representations, and mentally, including:*
  - *a two-digit number and tens.*

Add and subtract 2–digits and a multiple of ten (3)

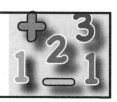

To solve the joke, write the answer to the maths question in the circle. Then use the grid to find the letter that goes with each answer and write it on the line. The first one is done for you!

58	93	37	67	39	66	83	89	52	62	16	96
T	R	N	A	S	I	J	V	E	M	P	L

What is sweet, red, sticky and bites people on the neck?

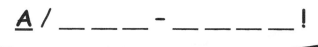

A / _ _ _ _ – _ _ _ _ _ !

17 + 50 = (**67**)

23 + 60 = (83)   97 – 30 = (67)   42 + 20 = (62) –

86 – 70 = (66)   46 + 20 = (66)   23 + 70 = (93)   72 – 20 = (52)

Year 2 – Addition and subtraction
* Add and subtract numbers using concrete objects, pictorial representations, and mentally, including:
  * a two-digit number and tens.

Add and subtract 2-digits and a multiple of ten (4)

Learning objectives
I can add a multiple of ten to a two-digit number.
I can subtract a multiple of ten from a two-digit number.

To solve the joke, write the answer to the maths question in the circle. Then use the grid to find the letter that goes with each answer and write it on the line. The first one is done for you!

58	93	37	67	39	66	83	89	52	62	16	96
T	R	N	A	S	I	J	V	E	M	P	L

What is a vampire's favourite ice-cream flavour?

<u>V</u> _ _ _ - _ _ _ _ !

39 + 50 = (**89**)   12 + 40 = ◯   86 − 20 = ◯   77 − 40 = ◯ −

16 + 50 = ◯   26 + 70 = ◯   56 + 40 = ◯   97 − 30 = ◯

Year 2 – Addition and subtraction
•   *Add and subtract numbers using concrete objects, pictorial representations, and mentally, including:*
   *   *a two-digit number and tens.*

Add and subtract 2-digits and a multiple of ten (5)

Learning objectives
I can add a multiple of ten to a two-digit number.
I can subtract a multiple of ten from a two-digit number.

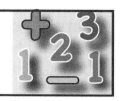

To solve the jokes, write the answer to the maths question in the circle. Then use the grid to find the letter that goes with each answer and write it on the line. The first one is done for you!

73	22	65	53	96	88	36	79	45	61	56	81
T	S	N	Y	E	A	O	I	U	M	R	P

What belongs to you but is used more often by other people?

Y _ _ _ / _ _ _ _ !

33 + 20 = (**53**)   86 − 50 = ◯   30 + 15 = ◯   96 − 40 = ◯

20 + 45 = ◯   38 + 50 = ◯   81 − 20 = ◯   66 + 30 = ◯

What flies but has no wings?

_ _ _ _ _ !

20 + 53 = ◯   99 − 20 = ◯   91 − 30 = ◯   26 + 70 = ◯

Year 2 – Addition and subtraction
- *Add and subtract numbers using concrete objects, pictorial representations, and mentally, including:*
  * *a two-digit number and tens.*

Add and subtract two 2-digit numbers (1)

Learning objectives
I can add two 2-digit numbers together.
I can subtract a 2-digit number from another 2-digit number.

To solve the joke, write the answer to the maths question in the circle. Then use the grid to find the letter that goes with each answer and write it on the line. The first one is done for you!

92	61	72	103	114	85	29	76	18	64	35	117
D	T	A	W	S	E	P	M	K	N	H	I

What do you give a poorly bird?

T _ _ _ _ _ - _ _ _ _ _ !

$37 + 24 =$ **61** $68 + 35 =$ ◯ $99 - 14 =$ ◯ $42 + 43 =$ ◯ $85 - 24 =$ ◯

$- \ 47 + 29 =$ ◯ $24 + 61 =$ ◯ $82 - 18 =$ ◯ $93 - 32 =$ ◯

Year 2 – Addition and subtraction
• *Add and subtract numbers using concrete objects, pictorial representations, and mentally, including:*
  * *two two-digit numbers.*

Add and subtract two 2-digit numbers (2)

Learning objectives
I can add two 2-digit numbers together.
I can subtract a 2-digit number from another 2-digit number.

To solve the joke, write the answer to the maths question in the circle. Then use the grid to find the letter that goes with each answer and write it on the line. The first one is done for you!

92	61	72	103	114	85	29	76	18	64	35	117
D	T	A	W	S	E	P	M	K	N	H	I

What is a parrot's favourite game?

H _ _ _ _ / _ _ _ _ / _ _ _ _ _ _ !

81 − 46 = ◯   82 + 35 = ◯   38 + 54 = ◯   61 + 24 = ◯

95 − 23 = ◯   91 − 27 = ◯   57 + 35 = ◯

31 + 83 = ◯   75 − 46 = ◯   67 + 18 = ◯   53 + 19 = ◯   67 − 49 = ◯

Year 2 – Addition and subtraction
•   *Add and subtract numbers using concrete objects, pictorial representations, and mentally, including:*
  ∗ two two-digit numbers.

Add and subtract two 2–digit numbers (3)

Learning objectives
I can add two 2-digit numbers together.
I can subtract a 2-digit number from another 2-digit number.

To solve the joke, write the answer to the maths question in the oval. Then use the grid to find the letter that goes with each answer and write it on the line. The first one is done for you!

135	24	89	57	46	35	65	108	52	81	61	97	13
M	Y	T	U	E	N	C	H	R	O	A	P	K

How would you describe a sad frog?

<u>U</u> _ - _ _ _ _ _ _ !

$22 + 35 =$ (**57**) $91 - 56 =$ ( ) $-$ $49 + 59 =$ ( )

$99 - 18 =$ ( ) $51 + 46 =$ ( ) $34 + 63 =$ ( ) $88 - 64 =$ ( )

Year 2 – Addition and subtraction
*   *Add and subtract numbers using concrete objects, pictorial representations, and mentally, including:*
*   *two two-digit numbers.*

Add and subtract two 2-digit numbers (4)

Learning objectives
I can add two 2-digit numbers together.
I can subtract a 2-digit number from another 2-digit number.

To solve the joke, write the answer to the maths question in the oval. Then use the grid to find the letter that goes with each answer and write it on the line. The first one is done for you!

135	24	89	57	46	35	65	108	52	81	61	97	13
M	Y	T	U	E	N	C	H	R	O	A	P	K

Where do frogs hang up their coats?

T _ _ / _ _ _ _ _ _ / _ _ _ _ !

67 + 22 = (**89**)   74 + 34 = ( )   85 – 39 = ( )

78 – 13 = ( )   98 – 46 = ( )   47 + 34 = ( )   43 + 18 = ( )   76 – 63 = ( )

81 – 29 = ( )   58 + 23 = ( )   42 + 39 = ( )   87 + 48 = ( )

Year 2 – Addition and subtraction
- *Add and subtract numbers using concrete objects, pictorial representations, and mentally, including:*
  * *two two-digit numbers.*

Add and subtract two 2-digit numbers (5)

Learning objectives
I can add two 2-digit numbers together.
I can subtract a 2-digit number from another 2-digit number.

To solve the jokes, write the answer to the maths question in the circle. Then use the grid to find the letter that goes with each answer and write it on the line. The first one is done for you!

164	22	86	57	159	15	96	61	28	107	172	113
O	W	C	V	L	E	P	R	F	S	I	T

What do you call a man with a seagull on his head?

C _ _ _ _ _ !

51 + 35 = (**86**)   83 + 76 = ( )   81 + 91 = ( )   85 − 57 = ( )   72 − 44 = ( )

Why was the broom late?

_ _ / _ _ _ _ _ -
_ _ _ _ _ !

87 + 85 = ( )   55 + 58 = ( )

76 + 88 = ( )   93 − 36 = ( )   73 − 58 = ( )   98 − 37 = ( ) −

43 + 64 = ( )   67 − 45 = ( )   56 − 41 = ( )   28 + 68 = ( )   56 + 57 = ( )

Year 2 – Addition and subtraction
•   *Add and subtract numbers using concrete objects, pictorial representations, and mentally, including:*
    *   *two two-digit numbers.*

Add three 1-digit numbers (1)

Learning objectives
I can add three 1-digit numbers together.

To solve the joke, write the answer to the maths question in the circle. Then use the grid to find the letter that goes with each answer and write it on the line. The first one is done for you!

23	9	6	17	21	14	20	24	13
Y	A	H	N	O	E	X	B	L

What did the bee say to his girlfriend?

<u>H</u> _ _ _ _ _ / _ _ _ _ _ _ !

$3 + 2 + 1 =$ (**6**) $5 + 2 + 7 =$ ( )

$6 + 3 + 4 =$ ( ) $8 + 2 + 3 =$ ( ) $7 + 9 + 5 =$ ( )

$2 + 4 + 0 =$ ( ) $9 + 8 + 4 =$ ( )

$6 + 8 + 3 =$ ( ) $6 + 5 + 3 =$ ( ) $8 + 9 + 6 =$ ( )

Year 2 – Addition and subtraction
•   *Add and subtract numbers using concrete objects, pictorial representations, and mentally, including:*
    * *two two-digit numbers.*

Add three 1–digit numbers (2)

Learning objectives
I can add three 1-digit numbers together.

To solve the joke, write the answer to the maths question in the circle. Then use the grid to find the letter that goes with each answer and write it on the line. The first one is done for you!

23	9	6	17	21	14	20	24	13
Y	A	H	N	O	E	X	B	L

$5 + 3 + 1 =$ ⑨

$2 + 2 + 2 =$ ◯ $7 + 8 + 6 =$ ◯

$9 + 3 + 5 =$ ◯ $1 + 9 + 4 =$ ◯ $8 + 8 + 7 =$ ◯

$6 + 9 + 9 =$ ◯ $9 + 3 + 9 =$ ◯ $8 + 7 + 5 =$ ◯

Year 2 – Addition and subtraction
* *Add and subtract numbers using concrete objects, pictorial representations, and mentally, including:*
  * *two two-digit numbers.*

Add three 1-digit numbers (3)

Learning objectives
I can add three 1-digit numbers together.

To solve the joke, write the answer to the maths question in the circle. Then use the grid to find the letter that goes with each answer and write it on the line. The first one is done for you!

22	16	14	15	18	13	19	20	24	26	17
T	A	M	Q	G	O	I	U	N	S	E

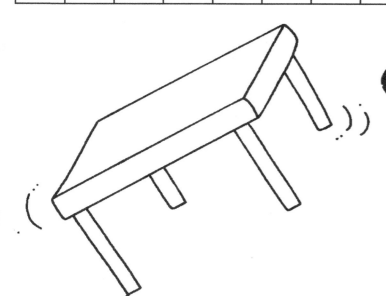

What kind of ant can lift a table?

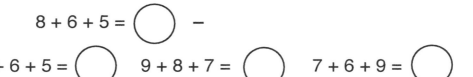

A / _ _ _ - _ _ _ _ !

$5 + 8 + 3 =$ (16)

$3 + 6 + 9 =$ ◯

$8 + 6 + 5 =$ ◯ –

$5 + 6 + 5 =$ ◯ $9 + 8 + 7 =$ ◯ $7 + 6 + 9 =$ ◯

Year 2 – Addition and subtraction
- *Add and subtract numbers using concrete objects, pictorial representations, and mentally, including:*
  - *two two-digit numbers.*

Add three 1-digit numbers (4)

Learning objectives
I can add three 1-digit numbers together.

To solve the joke, write the answer to the maths question in the circle. Then use the grid to find the letter that goes with each answer and write it on the line. The first one is done for you!

22	16	14	15	18	13	19	20	24	26	17
T	A	M	Q	G	O	I	U	N	S	E

What has antlers and sucks blood?

A / _ _ _ _ _ _ _ - _ _ _ _ _ !

9 + 2 + 5
= (**16**)

2 + 5 + 7
= ◯

6 + 3 + 4
= ◯

7 + 4 + 2
= ◯

9 + 9 + 8
= ◯

6 + 7 + 4
= ◯ −

8 + 3 + 4
= ◯

5 + 8 + 7
= ◯

9 + 3 + 7
= ◯

7 + 8 + 7
= ◯

8 + 1 + 4
= ◯

Year 2 – Addition and subtraction
- Add and subtract numbers using concrete objects, pictorial representations, and mentally, including:
  * three one-digit numbers.

Add three 1-digit numbers (5)

Learning objectives
I can add three 1-digit numbers together.

To solve the joke, write the answer to the maths question in the circle. Then use the grid to find the letter that goes with each answer and write it on the line. The first one is done for you!

13	19	22	18	23	17	16	12	25	14	20	15
E	T	B	R	A	F	L	I	O	S	C	M

What do you get if you cross a vampire with a snowman?

F _ _ _ _ _ / _ _ _ _ _ !

$5 + 4 + 8 =$ **17**

$8 + 6 + 4 =$ ◯

$9 + 7 + 9 =$ ◯

$2 + 7 + 5 =$ ◯

$9 + 7 + 3 =$ ◯

$8 + 6 + 8 =$ ◯

$3 + 5 + 4 =$ ◯

$8 + 4 + 7 =$ ◯

$6 + 2 + 5 =$ ◯

Year 2 – Addition and subtraction
- *Add and subtract numbers using concrete objects, pictorial representations, and mentally, including:*
  - * *three one-digit numbers.*

Add three 1-digit numbers (6)

Learning objectives
I can add three 1-digit numbers together.

To solve the joke, write the answer to the maths question in the circle. Then use the grid to find the letter that goes with each answer and write it on the line. The first one is done for you!

13	19	22	18	23	17	16	12	25	14	20	15
E	T	B	R	A	F	L	I	O	S	C	M

What has two humps and is found at the North Pole?

A / _ _ _ _ _ / _ _ _ _ _ _ !

$7 + 9 + 7 =$ (**23**)

$6 + 1 + 9 =$ ◯ $7 + 9 + 9 =$ ◯ $1 + 8 + 5 =$ ◯ $5 + 7 + 7 =$ ◯

$9 + 2 + 9 =$ ◯ $8 + 7 + 8 =$ ◯

$5 + 4 + 6 =$ ◯ $2 + 7 + 4 =$ ◯ $8 + 1 + 7 =$ ◯

Year 2 – Addition and subtraction
- *Add and subtract numbers using concrete objects, pictorial representations, and mentally, including:*
  - *three one-digit numbers.*

Add and subtract missing number inverse (1)

Learning objectives
I know that addition and subtraction are the inverse of each other – they are opposites.
I can solve missing number questions using the inverse.

To solve the joke, use the inverse to work out what number needs to go in the circle to make the number sentence correct. Then use the grid to find the letter that goes with each answer and write it on the line. The first one is done for you!

65	50	9	6	40	8	56	7	14	5	93	32	37	4
T	U	A	N	E	C	L	B	O	M	D	R	H	S

What type of dog does Dracula have?

<u>A</u> / _ _ _ _ _ _ / _ _ _ _ _ !

$15 - \boxed{9} = 6$

$33 - \bigcirc = 26$ $\bigcirc - 20 = 36$ $12 + \bigcirc = 26$ $21 - \bigcirc = 7$ $\bigcirc - 60 = 33$

$35 + \bigcirc = 72$ $50 - \bigcirc = 36$ $85 - \bigcirc = 35$ $52 - \bigcirc = 46$ $\bigcirc - 8 = 85$

Year 2 – Addition and subtraction
- *Recognise and use the inverse relationship between addition and subtraction and use this to check calculations and solve missing number problems.*

Add and subtract missing number inverse (2)

Learning objectives
I know that addition and subtraction are the inverse of each other – they are opposites.
I can solve missing number questions using the inverse.

To solve the joke, use the inverse to work out what number needs to go in the circle to make the number sentence correct. Then use the grid to find the letter that goes with each answer and write it on the line. The first one is done for you!

65	50	9	6	40	8	56	7	14	5	93	32	37	4
T	U	A	N	E	C	L	B	O	M	D	R	H	S

Which trees do vampires like best?

C _ _ _ _ _ - _ _ _ _ _ _ !

$8 + 7 + \boxed{8} = 23$

$54 - \bigcirc = 14$

$\bigcirc + 9 + 5 = 19$

$\bigcirc + 16 = 56$ $-$

$82 - \bigcirc = 17$

$\bigcirc - 18 = 14$

$83 - \bigcirc = 43$

$\bigcirc + 59 = 99$

$82 - \bigcirc = 78$

Year 2 – Addition and subtraction
• *Recognise and use the inverse relationship between addition and subtraction and use this to check calculations and solve missing number problems.*

Add and subtract missing number inverse (3)

Learning objectives
I know that addition and subtraction are the inverse of each other – they are opposites.
I can solve missing number questions using the inverse.

To solve the joke, use the inverse to work out what number needs to go in the circle to make the number sentence correct. Then use the grid to find the letter that goes with each answer and write it on the line. The first one is done for you!

7	35	8	18	6	9	47	20	70	50
S	L	A	O	N	M	D	T	E	R

What type of snake is good at maths?

A __ / __ __ __ __ __ __ !

$39 - \boxed{8} = 31$ $\bigcirc + 5 + 9 = 20$

$52 - \bigcirc = 44$ $\bigcirc + 20 = 67$ $\bigcirc - 19 = 28$ $\bigcirc + 27 = 97$ $82 - \bigcirc = 32$

Year 2 – Addition and subtraction
• *Recognise and use the inverse relationship between addition and subtraction and use this to check calculations and solve missing number problems.*

Add and subtract missing number inverse (4)

Learning objectives
I know that addition and subtraction are the inverse of each other –
they are opposites.
I can solve missing number questions using the inverse.

To solve the joke, use the inverse to work out what number needs to go in the circle to make the number sentence correct. Then use the grid to find the letter that goes with each answer and write it on the line. The first one is done for you!

7	35	8	18	6	9	47	20	70	50
S	L	A	O	N	M	D	T	E	R

Which hand should you use to pick up a poisonous snake?

S _ _ _ _ _ _ _ / _ _ _ _ _ ' _ !

$9 + 8 + \bigcirc{7} = 24$ $67 + \bigcirc = 85$ $\bigcirc + 9 + 7 = 25$ $96 - \bigcirc = 26$

$50 + \bigcirc = 68$ $5 + 8 + \bigcirc = 19$ $13 + \bigcirc = 83$

$75 - \bigcirc = 5$ $54 + \bigcirc = 89$ $85 + \bigcirc = 92$ $21 + \bigcirc = 91$

$64 - \bigcirc = 57$

Year 2 – Addition and subtraction
* *Recognise and use the inverse relationship between addition and subtraction and use this to check calculations and solve missing number problems.*

Add and subtract missing number inverse (5)

To solve the joke, use the inverse to work out what number needs to go in the circle to make the number sentence correct. Then use the grid to find the letter that goes with each answer and write it on the line. The first one is done for you!

28	5	60	37	8	20	49	7	30	6	22
P	T	A	H	R	I	M	C	E	W	S

What do cats read in the mornings?

T _ _ / _ _ _ _ _ - _ _ _ _ _ _ !

$7 + 8 + \boxed{5} = 20$ $52 + \bigcirc = 89$ $28 + \bigcirc = 58$

$51 + \bigcirc = 100$ $78 - \bigcirc = 48$ $\bigcirc + 8 + 5 = 19$ $68 - \bigcirc = 46$ –

$35 + \bigcirc = 63$ $78 - \bigcirc = 18$ $\bigcirc + 20 = 48$ $\bigcirc + 36 = 66$

$\bigcirc + 2 + 9 = 19$

Year 2 – Addition and subtraction
* *Recognise and use the inverse relationship between addition and subtraction and use this to check calculations and solve missing number problems.*

Add and subtract missing number inverse (6)

To solve the joke, use the inverse to work out what number needs to go in the circle
to make the number sentence correct. Then use the grid to find the letter that goes
with each answer and write it on the line. The first on is done for you!

28	5	60	37	8	20	49	7	30	6	22
P	T	A	A	H	R	I	M	C	W	S

What did the cat make when he locked a mouse in the freezer?

M _ _ _ / _ _ _ _ _ _ !

$42 + \bigcirc 49 = 91$

$52 + \bigcirc = 72$

$5 + 8 + \bigcirc = 20$

$\bigcirc - 11 = 19$

$73 - \bigcirc = 66$

$87 + \bigcirc = 95$

$74 - \bigcirc = 44$

$\bigcirc + 27 = 87$

$\bigcirc + 27 = 76$

Year 2 – Addition and subtraction
* Recognise and use the inverse relationship between addition and subtraction and use this to check calculations and solve missing number problems.

Multiples of 2, 5 and 10 (1)

Learning objectives
I can answer questions in the 2, 5 and 10 times tables.
I know or can work out related divisions for the 2, 5 and 10
   times tables.

To solve the joke, write the answer to the maths question in the circle. Then use the grid to find the letter that goes with each answer and write it on the line. The first one is done for you!

6	60	18	35	12	10	8	40	70	45	100
T	R	G	E	O	A	C	D	K	Y	L

How do teddy bears start a race?

R _ _ _ _ _ / _ _ _ _ _ _ / _ _ !

10 x 6 = (60)   7 x 5 = ◯   20 ÷ 2 = ◯   4 x 10 = ◯   9 x 5 = ◯

30 ÷ 5 = ◯   5 x 7 = ◯   10 x 4 = ◯   8 x 5 = ◯   5 x 9 = ◯

9 x 2 = ◯   24 ÷ 2 = ◯

Year 2 – Multiplication and division
•   *Recall and use multiplication and division facts for the 2, 5 and 10 multiplication tables, including:*
   *   *recognising odd and even numbers.*

Multiples of 2, 5 and 10 (2)

Learning objectives
I can answer questions in the 2, 5 and 10 times tables.
I know or can work out related divisions for the 2, 5 and 10
  times tables.

To solve the joke, write the answer to the maths question in the circle. Then use the grid to find the letter that goes with each answer and write it on the line. The first one is done for you!

6	60	18	35	12	10	8	40	70	45	100
T	R	G	E	O	A	C	D	K	Y	L

What is a bear's favourite drink?

$\underline{C}$ _ _ _ _ / _ _ _ _ _ _ !

$40 \div 5 =$ (**8**)

$6 \times 2 =$ ◯

$80 \div 10 =$ ◯

$50 \div 5 =$ ◯

$10 \times 7 =$ ◯

$60 \div 5 =$ ◯

$5 \times 2 =$ ◯

$10 \times 10 =$ ◯

$100 \div 10 =$ ◯

Year 2 – Multiplication and division
* *Recall and use multiplication and division facts for the 2, 5 and 10 multiplication tables, including:*
  * *recognising odd and even numbers.*

Multiples of 2, 5 and 10 (3)

To solve the jokes, write the answer to the maths question in the circle. Then use the grid to find the letter that goes with each answer and write it on the line. The first one is done for you!

20	80	7	30	6	15	1	3	5
K	S	M	A	T	C	L	P	O

What has hands and a face, but no arms or legs?

<u>A</u> / _ _ _ _ _ _ !

$10 \times 3 = $ **30**

$5 \times 3 = \bigcirc$ $10 \div 10 = \bigcirc$ $25 \div 5 = \bigcirc$ $3 \times 5 = \bigcirc$ $2 \times 10 = \bigcirc$

What goes around the world but stays in a corner?

_ / _ _ _ _ _ _ !

$5 \times 6 = \bigcirc$

$10 \times 8 = \bigcirc$ $30 \div 5 = \bigcirc$ $3 \times 10 = \bigcirc$ $14 \div 2 = \bigcirc$ $30 \div 10 = \bigcirc$

Year 2 – Multiplication and division
- *Recall and use multiplication and division facts for the 2, 5 and 10 multiplication tables, including:*
  * *recognising odd and even numbers.*

Multiples of 2, 5 and 10 (4)

Learning objectives
I can answer questions in the 2, 5 and 10 times tables.
I know or can work out related divisions for the 2, 5 and 10
   times tables.

To solve the joke, write the answer to the maths question in the circle. Then use the grid to find the letter that goes with each answer and write it on the line. The first one is done for you!

50	25	30	2	40	55	4	100	1	9	7	90
I	D	T	S	U	H	N	W	A	O	F	Q

What type of fish are best at singing?

T _ _ _ _ / _ _ _ _ _ !

$3 \times 10 =$ (**30**) $5 \times 8 =$ ◯ $20 \div 5 =$ ◯ $2 \div 2 =$ ◯

$70 \div 10 =$ ◯ $10 \times 5 =$ ◯ $4 \div 2 =$ ◯ $11 \times 5 =$ ◯

Year 2 – Multiplication and division
- *Recall and use multiplication and division facts for the 2, 5 and 10 multiplication tables, including:*
  - * *recognising odd and even numbers.*

Multiples of 2, 5 and 10 (5)

Learning objectives
I can answer questions in the 2, 5 and 10 times tables.
I know or can work out related divisions for the 2, 5 and 10
   times tables.

To solve the joke, write the answer to the maths question in the circle. Then use the grid to find the letter that goes with each answer and write it on the line. The first one is done for you!

50	25	30	2	40	55	4	100	1	9	7	90
I	D	T	S	U	H	N	W	A	O	F	Q

How much did the octopus
spend at the shop?

T _ _ / _ _ _ _ _ _ !

5 x 6 = (**30**)   10 x 10 = ◯   45 ÷ 5 = ◯

20 ÷ 10 = ◯   10 x 9 = ◯   8 x 5 = ◯

                        5 x 10 = ◯   5 x 5 = ◯

Year 2 – Multiplication and division
*   *Recall and use multiplication and division facts for the 2, 5 and 10 multiplication tables, including:*
    *   *recognising odd and even numbers.*

Multiplication and division problems (1)

Learning objectives

I can use repeated addition, pictures, arrays or times tables to help me multiply two numbers.

I can use grouping, sharing or times tables to help me divide numbers.

I know the language of multiplication and division.

To solve the joke, work out the answer to each question and write it in the circle. Then use the grid to find the letter that goes with each answer and write it on the line. The first one is done for you!

6	8	18	5	12	10	4	40	70	45	100
S	C	T	O	F	L	R	D	M	E	N

How many groups of 2 are in 16? (**8**)

Share 50 equally between 5. ( )

What is 1 group of 5? ( )

What is 9 lots of 5? ( )

How many lots of 2 are in 10? ( )

What is 10 multiplied by 4? ( )

What is 10 times 10? ( )

How many lots of 2 are in 12? ( )

Year 2 – Multiplication and division
- *Solve problems involving multiplication and division, using materials, arrays, repeated addition, mental methods, and multiplication and division facts, including:*
  - ** problems in context.*

Multiplication and division problems (2)

Learning objectives

I can use repeated addition, pictures, arrays or times tables to help me multiply two numbers.
I can use grouping, sharing or times tables to help me divide numbers.
I know the language of multiplication and division.

To solve the joke, work out the answer to each question and write it in the circle. Then use the grid to find the letter that goes with each answer and write it on the line. The first one is done for you!

6	8	18	5	12	10	4	40	70	45	100
S	C	T	O	F	L	R	D	M	E	N

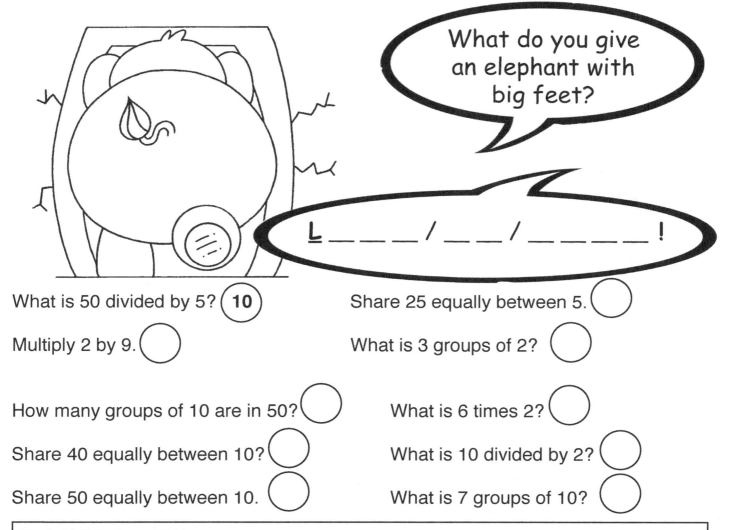

What do you give an elephant with big feet?

L _ _ _ _ / _ _ / _ _ _ _ !

What is 50 divided by 5? (**10**)   Share 25 equally between 5. ◯

Multiply 2 by 9. ◯   What is 3 groups of 2? ◯

How many groups of 10 are in 50? ◯   What is 6 times 2? ◯

Share 40 equally between 10? ◯   What is 10 divided by 2? ◯

Share 50 equally between 10. ◯   What is 7 groups of 10? ◯

Year 2 – Multiplication and division
* *Solve problems involving multiplication and division, using materials, arrays, repeated addition, mental methods, and multiplication and division facts, including:*
  * *problems in context.*

Multiplication and division problems (3)

Learning objectives
I can use repeated addition, pictures, arrays or times tables to help me multiply two numbers.
I can use grouping, sharing or times tables to help me divide numbers.
I know the language of multiplication and division.

To solve the joke, work out the answer to each question and write it in the circle. Then use the grid to find the letter that goes with each answer and write it on the line. The first one is done for you!

20	80	7	30	6	15	1	3	5	4	12	60
G	K	E	S	A	T	R	H	W	Y	I	C

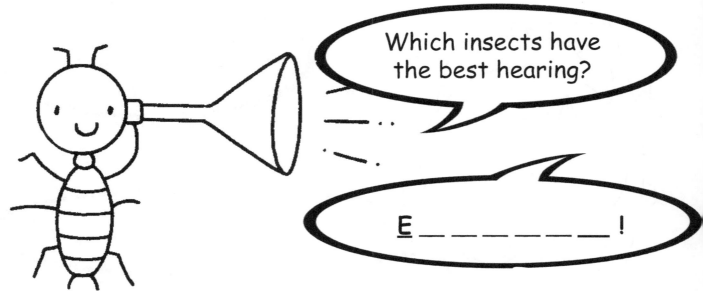

Which insects have the best hearing?

E _ _ _ _ _ _ _ _ !

How many groups of 2 are in 14? (**7**)   Share 12 equally between 2. ◯

What is 10 divided by 10? ◯

How many lots of 5 are in 25? ◯   Multiply 6 by 2. ◯

What is 10 groups of 2? ◯   What is 6 times 5? ◯

Year 2 – Multiplication and division
- *Solve problems involving multiplication and division, using materials, arrays, repeated addition, mental methods, and multiplication and division facts, including:*
  - ** problems in context.*

Multiplication and division problems (4)

Learning objectives
I can use repeated addition, pictures, arrays or times tables to help me multiply two numbers.
I can use grouping, sharing or times tables to help me divide numbers.
I know the language of multiplication and division.

To solve the joke, work out the answer to each question and write it in the circle. Then use the grid to find the letter that goes with each answer and write it on the line. The first one is done for you!

20	80	7	30	6	15	1	3	5	4	12	60
G	K	E	S	A	T	R	H	W	Y	I	C

How do fleas travel from one place to another?

T _ _ _ _ /
_ _ _ _ _ / _ _ _ _ _ !

What is 3 lots of 5? (**15**)

What is 14 divided by 2? ◯

What is 2 groups of 6? ◯

What is 6 times 10? ◯

Divide 15 by 5. ◯

What is 8 lots of 10? ◯

Share 30 equally between 10. ◯

How many groups of 5 are in 20? ◯

Multiply 5 by 3. ◯

Share 6 equally between 2. ◯

How many groups of 2 are in 24? ◯

How many lots of 5 are in 35? ◯

Year 2 – Multiplication and division
- *Solve problems involving multiplication and division, using materials, arrays, repeated addition, mental methods, and multiplication and division facts, including:*
  - ** problems in context.*

Multiplication and division problems (5)

Learning objectives
I can use repeated addition, pictures, arrays or times tables to help me multiply two numbers.
I can use grouping, sharing or times tables to help me divide numbers.
I know the language of multiplication and division.

To solve the joke, work out the answer to each question and write it in the circle. Then use the grid to find the letter that goes with each answer and write it on the line. The first one is done for you!

50	25	30	100	40	55	2	4	1	9	7	90
T	S	I	W	D	N	A	E	V	R	Y	K

What hairstyle does the sea have?

W _ _ _ _ !

What is 10 lots of 10? **(100)**

What is 5 divided by 5? ◯

How many groups of 2 are in 4? ◯

Share 35 equally between 5. ◯

Year 2 – Multiplication and division
- *Solve problems involving multiplication and division, using materials, arrays, repeated addition, mental methods, and multiplication and division facts, including problems in context.*

Multiplication and division problems (6)

Learning objectives
I can use repeated addition, pictures, arrays or times tables to help me multiply two numbers.
I can use grouping, sharing or times tables to help me divide numbers.
I know the language of multiplication and division.

To solve the joke, work out the answer to each question and write it in the circle. Then use the grid to find the letter that goes with each answer and write it on the line. The first one is done for you!

50	25	30	100	40	55	2	4	1	9	7	90
T	S	I	W	D	N	A	E	V	R	Y	K

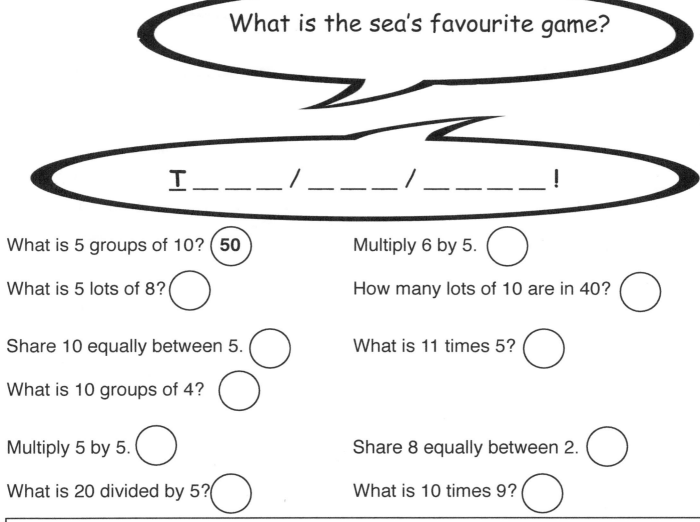

What is the sea's favourite game?

T _ _ _ _ / _ _ _ _ / _ _ _ _ _ !

What is 5 groups of 10? (50)

What is 5 lots of 8? ( )

Share 10 equally between 5. ( )

What is 10 groups of 4? ( )

Multiply 5 by 5. ( )

What is 20 divided by 5? ( )

Multiply 6 by 5. ( )

How many lots of 10 are in 40? ( )

What is 11 times 5? ( )

Share 8 equally between 2. ( )

What is 10 times 9? ( )

Year 2 – Multiplication and division
•   *Solve problems involving multiplication and division, using materials, arrays, repeated addition, mental methods, and multiplication and division facts, including problems in context.*

Recognise fractions (1)

Learning objectives
I can write how much of a shape is shaded as a fraction.
I can find fractions of a number or set of objects.
I know that ½ is equivalent to ²/₄.

To solve the jokes, work out what fraction of the shape is shaded. Write the answer in the oval then use the grid to find the letter that goes with each answer and write it on the line. The first one is done for you!

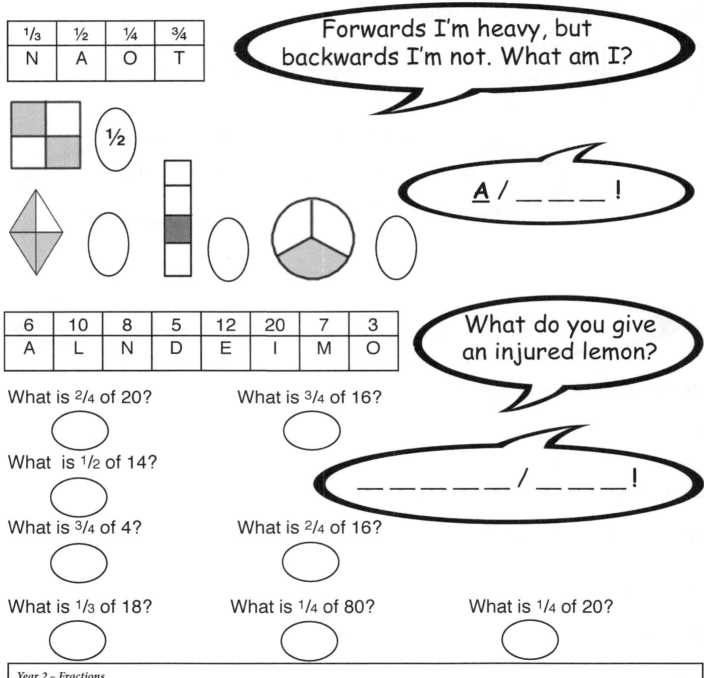

¹/₃	½	¼	¾
N	A	O	T

Forwards I'm heavy, but backwards I'm not. What am I?

½

A / _ _ _ _ !

6	10	8	5	12	20	7	3
A	L	N	D	E	I	M	O

What is ²/₄ of 20?

What is ³/₄ of 16?

What do you give an injured lemon?

What is ¹/₂ of 14?

_ _ _ _ _ _ / _ _ _ _ !

What is ³/₄ of 4?

What is ²/₄ of 16?

What is ¹/₃ of 18?

What is ¹/₄ of 80?

What is ¹/₄ of 20?

Year 2 – Fractions
•   *Recognise, find, name and write fractions 1/3, 1/4, 2/4 and 3/4 of a length, shape, set of objects or quantity*
•   *Write simple fractions, for example, ½ of 6 = 3, and recognise the equivalence of 1/2 and 2/4.*

Recognise fractions (2)

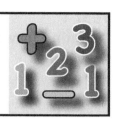

To solve the jokes, work out what fraction of the shape is shaded. Write the answer in the oval then use the grid to find the letter that goes with each answer and write it on the line.

¹/3	½	¼	³/4
Y	U	L	G

What do you call a creature with two heads, six arms, five eyes and one leg?

_ _ _ _ _ _ !

5	6	30	15	20	4
M	A	K	L	S	E

Which vegetable is always getting wet?

_ _ / _ _ _ _ _ !

What is ¹/4 of 24?

What is ³/4 of 20?

What is ¹/3 of 12?

What is ²/4 of 8?   What is ³/4 of 40?

Year 2 – Fractions
*   *Recognise, find, name and write fractions 1/3, 1/4, 2/4 and 3/4 of a length, shape, set of objects or quantity*
*   *Write simple fractions, for example, ½ of 6 = 3, and recognise the equivalence of 1/2 and 2/4.*

Answers

Year 1

Counting forwards and backwards in ones

Activity 1	100, 60, 80, 99, 66, 102, 19, 19	HEL-MUTT!	5
	98, 102, 98, 71, 40, 101, 29	PUP-CORN!	
Activity 2	80, 100, 99, 80, 100, 99, 19, 100	A DEAD-END!	6
	19, 50, 59, 50, 100, 29	NO-BODY!	
Activity 3	99, 100, 19, 70, 49, 40, 99, 68, 80	A FISH-TANK!	7
	99, 100, 101, 99, 40, 100, 19, 70, 49	A FLAT FISH!	

Counting in multiples of 2, 5 and 10

Activity 1	12, 40, 30, 20	COAL!	8
	60, 40, 16, 90, 50, 58, 70	YOUR BED!	
Activity 2	28, 80, 40, 70	SNAP!	9
	40, 58, 40, 12, 60, 70, 90, 34, 22	A LAMB-PIRE!	
Activity 3	90, 60, 10, 30, 90, 80, 44, 100	THEY TIDE!	10
	80, 22, 90, 60, 100, 70, 35, 50, 30	IN THE ARMY!	

One more or one less

Activity 1	20, 29, 69, 38, 9, 73	A CLOUD!	11
	48, 20, 20, 69, 69, 59, 100	BAA-LLET!	
Activity 2	50, 19, 50, 99, 35, 69, 17, 19, 80, 35	AN ASTRO-NUT!	12
	99, 35, 50, 69, 99	STARS!	
Activity 3	80, 25, 25, 80, 69, 69, 34, 100, 80, 30	TOOTH-HURTY!	13
	19, 10, 75, 20, 20	GLASS!	

Reading numbers

Activity 1	17, 9, 8, 13, 5, 6, 19, 12, 8, 6, 11, 5	A LIGHTS-WITCH!	14
Activity 2	9, 10, 2, 20, 10, 9, 12, 17, 2	A TENT-ACLE!	15
Activity 3	12, 14, 16, 7, 18, 12, 1, 3, 16, 5	ONE, TWO, FLEA!	16

Writing numbers

Activity 1	seven, sixteen, sixteen, twenty,		
	four, three, fourteen, seven, one, eighteen	GOOD FRIGHT!	17
Activity 2	fifteen, three, five, sixteen, three,		
	seven, thirteen, eleven	DOC TOPUS!	18
Activity 3	eleven, nineteen, eleven, eight, nine, nine	BY BUZZ!	19

+ and − bonds to 20

Activity 1	2, 11, 9, 2, 6, 3	A CHAIR!	20
	2, 9, 8, 12, 13	A HOLE!	
Activity 2	20, 4, 16, 7, 9, 4, 16, 7	MARS BARS!	21
	7, 18, 4, 16, 13, 15, 7, 1	STAR-FISH!	
Activity 3	3, 6, 19, 0, 1, 1, 4	THE DOOR!	22
	18, 1, 12, 0, 17, 3	FOLD IT!	

+ and − within 20

Activity 1	3, 7, 19, 3, 14	A ROAD!	23
	3, 12, 6, 3, 16	A FLAG!	
Activity 2	6, 9, 9, 17, 9, 15, 13	MOO YORK!	24
	20, 6, 9, 9, 19, 16, 11, 6	A MOO-SEUM!	
Activity 3	18, 7, 5, 3, 9, 16, 8, 5, 10, 16, 11	THE SPACE BAR!	25
	13, 5, 9, 18, 14, 13, 5, 3	NEP-TUNES!	

Assessment checklist

Put a ✔ in the box when the pupil has successfully completed the activity.

Name _____   Class _____

Year 1

	1	2	3	4	5	6
Counting forwards and backwards in ones						
Counting in multiples of 2, 5 and 10						
One more or one less						
Reading numbers						
Writing numbers						
+ and – bonds to 20						
+ and – within 20						
Simple multiplication and division						

Year 2

	1	2	3	4	5	6
Counting forwards and backwards in steps of 2, 3, 5 and 10						
Place, value tens and ones						
Reading numbers to 100						
Writing numbers to 100						
Number facts to 20 and 10s to 100						
Add and subtract 2-digit and 1-digit						
Add and subtract 2-digits and a multiple of ten						
Add and subtract two 2-digit numbers						
Add three 1-digit numbers						
Add, subtract missing number inverse						
Multiples of 2, 5 and 10						
Multiplication and division problems						
Recognise fractions						

Lightning Source UK Ltd.
Milton Keynes UK
UKOW06f2123290914

239359UK00001B/12/P

9 781783 170838